The Joys of
Smoking Cigarettes

HARPER 💬 ENTERTAINMENT

NEW YORK · LONDON · TORONTO · SYDNEY

The Joys of
Smoking Cigarettes

James Fitzgerald

HARPER ● ENTERTAINMENT

Grateful acknowledgment is made to the following for the use of the illustrations and photographs that appear in this book: Pages 8, 11, 16, 17, 18, 19, 20, 21, 67, 68, 87, 94, 98, 99, 100, 101, 104, 105, 106, 107, 109, 110, 111, 112, 113, 114, 124, 125, 136, 157, 158, 161, and 162: Harvey Wang. Pages 41, 57, 63, 66, 70, 73, 77, 78, 82, 87, 89, 91, 93, 119, 121, 131, 133, 146, 154, and 168: Rob Dobi. Pages ii–iii, vii, 13, 35, 36, 50, 51, 52, 54, 58, 62, 73, 95, 96, 97, 126, and 145: Associated Press/UPI. Pages i, v, x, 14, 15, 47, 55, 71, 74, 75, 76, 85, 103, 144, 150, and 167: Library of Congress. Pages vi, 44, 45, 83, 92, 134, 152, and 155: R. J. Reynolds. Pages 47, 52, 53, 54, 55, 81, 97, 115, 132, and 164: Getty Images. Pages 39, 48, 49, 54, 61, 116, and 153: Liggett & Meyers. Pages 56 and 108: P. Lorillard Co. Pages 1, 30, 64, 84, 123, 129, 130, 160, and 174: James Fitzgerald Archive. Pages 42 and 43: SFNTC. Page 34: Elmer Napier. Page 79: Philip Morris. Page 96: Acme. Pages 122 and 125: The American Tobacco Co. Page 125: New York Journal. Page 151: International News Photo. Pages: 172 and 173: B&W T Co. Pages: 93 and 123: Al Kilgore.

This book was originally published in 1983 by Holt, Rinehart & Winston.

HarperCollins books may be purchased for educational, business, or sales promotional use. For information please write: Special Markets Department, HarperCollins Publishers, 10 East 53rd Street, New York, NY 10022.

First Harper Entertainment paperback published 2007.

Designed by Justin Dodd

Library of Congress Cataloging-in-Publication Data has been applied for.

ISBN: 987-0-06-125227-3 (pbk.)
ISBN-10: 0-06-125227-1 (pbk.)

07 08 09 10 11 ID/RRD 10 9 8 7 6 5 4 3 2 1

This book is dedicated to that
little bit of Indian that resides
in every smoker on earth.

Contents

"Smoking takes ten years off your life. Well, it's the ten worst years, isn't it, folks? It's the ones at the end! It's the wheelchair-kidney-dialysis-fucking years. You can have those years! We don't want 'em, all right!? And with that in mind, light up, everyone, and have a good day."

—Denis Leary

Street urchins no doubt and perhaps of the ones who inhabited lower Manhattan during the Jacob Riis–period of the late-nineteenth century. They all look so tough and very grown-up with their cigarettes. According to Luc Sante in his book *Low Life: Lures and Snares of Old New York*, there were 20 to 30,000 homeless children in Manhattan alone in 1876. In 2007 terms that is a city roughly the size of modern-day Taos, New Mexico.

Introduction

A book entitled *The Joys of Smoking Cigarettes* should rightfully begin with the history of cigarettes in my short untethered life.

Pop

My mother's father, that would be my grandfather, whom we simply called "Pop," smoked a pipe. I never actually saw him smoke it; he wasn't a ruminating "Sit down here, sonny, and I'll tell you about the time . . ." type, but there was a virtual armada of pipes around, some of them mixed in with my electric train cars and make-believe tools, all smelling ancient, cavelike, European, feral—like the horse farms in Denmark; not that I had been to Denmark yet, but that was where Pop was from. I saw him with a cigar, I think, once or twice in real time, but all the black-and-white photographs of him standing by some northern midwestern lake in suspenders with my Shirley Temple—dressed mother high atop one of his shoulders always included a cigar that looked like it had been surgically attached to the right side of his mouth. He was a smoker, but not a modern one.

And of course both of my parents smoked. They were part of that whole tribe of white Americans who all seemed to celebrate the end of the Second World War by moving to the suburbs, buying collies and Chryslers, shopping in well-lighted department stores, drinking gin and tonics in the backyard while the kids watched television inside, and . . . they all smoked cigarettes. And why not? The late '40s and '50s ushered in

1

a host of new brands and flavors: Salems, like the great out-of-doors, were mentholated; Herbert Tareytons suggested authority and old school−ness; Parliaments had their recessed filters; Kents, which all the young new doctors seemed to smoke, had micronite filters— the list of choices seemed to go on and on. Suburban cigarettes. And people smoked everywhere and at any time. Big finned cars featured Montana-sized ashtrays with push-button cigarette lighters in both the front and backseats. Some of the high-ticket cars, like the Caddies and Imperials, had as many as four ashtray-lighter combos scattered around their cockpits. People smoked on television, on airplanes, buses, and trains, in banks and supermarkets, on playing fields, everywhere. It seems as if I was born into a P. J. Lorillard hospital and grew up in the R. J. Reynolds playing fields. Americans had won the war and were prosperous. They were smoking cigarettes to prove it.

As a child I was aware of cigarettes, but they weren't part of my life, as they later came to be. As noted earlier, my parents smoked, but my surrogate parents, my aunt and uncle, didn't. I was too young and didn't see the subtle differences between the two couples. I thought my parents were naughty and worldly and smoked, and my aunt and uncle were good and abiding and didn't smoke. Our yardman smoked cigarettes after lunch down by the garage, and the maids, who did not smoke (or at least I never saw them smoking), would giggle at his jokes as the smoke curled its way out of his nose. I was fascinated by him, his yellow fingers, and his weirdly small cigarettes that had a name something like Faros.

Even though we children would complain about all the cigarette smoke in the house, the car, the yard, we would, just to make our parents feel grounded, I guess, beg them for cigarette tricks. There was one my father would do when he had imbibed on certain occasions. He would gobble a whole cigarette before our eyes. The collies would bark at him and the maids again would giggle in the wings, and he would be left with a mouth full of tobacco. We thought it was hilarious and stupid.

My mother, being the ultra-modern '50s woman she was, followed every fashion and folly that magazines and television had to offer, ranging from rinsing away the oil stains in the driveway with Tang to storing cartons of her menthol cigarettes in the freezer right alongside the boxes of chicken pot pies and Lik-Em-Stix. "Keeps them fresh," she claimed.

My lasting image of cigarettes as a child, though, was watching the gentle glow of a discarded butt in the grass as we fell asleep in our parents' arms at late-night dinner parties in our backyard.

As a freshman at a go-away high school, I called home about two weeks in, with an urgent request. I really was homesick, but I ostensibly called to complain about my roommate. I wanted a new roommate because the one I had seemed to be much older than me, and he was from Mexico and had little command of the English language. The language part didn't bother me, but what really did was that he smoked cigarettes. The shock of going away was enough, but to be locked away in a bunk-bedded dorm room with a smoker was too much. I was in my sports years, my body was changing, and there was no room for tobacco yet. My wish was granted. I was given a new roommate, who, instead of lying on the bottom bunk smoking cigarettes, would lie there in his undershorts asking me things like, "Think they'll serve mystery meat again for dinner?" or what the chances were of just seeing (no way would we ever talk to) a certain blonde and bouncy cheerleader type from our sister school at the mixer on Friday night.

By the end of the year, I couldn't decide whom I disdained more, my nonsmoking second roommate from Ohio, the boring idealist with pimples and a slew of Irish brothers who he would follow in his predictable footsteps and end up working at their father's cement conversion plant, or the mustachioed Mexican pragmatist who had decided that he and his cigarettes were his answer to society. So I forgot about both of them.

The summer following my freshman year I entered the first phase of the becoming-a-man cycle. No longer did I expect or want to wait for my allowance to be doled out, only to then run to the shopping center like a cocker spaniel off a leash to hang out with the other kids from the neighborhood. I was kind of working. Kind of. It was an odd setup: a drive-in grocery store where you actually drove your car through the store, pointing out or shouting to the attendants which items you wanted. The attendants, of which I was one, would scamper about selecting items and placing them on a tray that was attached to the driver's window. The majority of the customers were the beer-cigarette-soda-and-milk crowd with a few dog food buyers thrown in, but we did get some odd requests, my favorite coming from an older gentleman who pulled in and requested eggnog. (It was summertime in Texas!) I started handling cigarettes a lot then. People would drive in smoking cigarettes and order cigarettes. It was an older person's habit, I thought.

That same summer, a fellow freshman, soon to be a sophomore, was in town and called me from the swanky new motel on the highway. He said he'd pick me up and we'd get some lunch. It was my day off. In my madras shorts, T-shirt, and Jack Purcells, I sat with him around the swimming pool eating turkey clubs, drinking ginger ale, and questioning the merits of everything from a classmate's record collection to the Kennedy administration. We were both acting very grown-up.

The day progressed. My friend had a knack with the opposite sex, and before I knew it we were going on a date that evening with two fellow swimmers we had met near the pool earlier. They both covered their mouths when they giggled. He had told them we were in college, blah blah blah. . . . I was nervous and would rather have stayed at home reading *Sports Illustrated* or watching *Bonanza* on TV, but my time of teenage chivalry had arrived. I decided I had to go.

4

My friend knew of my neophyte status in such affairs, so he prepped me. Do this, say that, when he winked it meant the time had come for me and my date to disappear, but what I garnered most from his older teenage wisdom was "Hold a cigarette. You don't have to smoke it, but it makes you look older, like you're in college."

So, sitting in the backseat of a Buick convertible with my new girlfriend Brenda on a hot summer night, overlooking the Rio Grande, I lit my first cigarette and thought I looked like I was in college. By the end of the evening I had confessed my real status and had eased the conversation into the familiar grounds of rock and roll and movies. Still, I was convinced that the cigarette I was holding made me look and feel more grown-up. I had smoked, or rather held, the whole pack before the evening was over.

My interest and participation in sports for the next two years kept me from the evil weed. Cigarettes were for a small minority that went to a roped-off area on "the hill." Cigarettes were for seniors who were nervous about college and smoked in their rooms after lights out. Cigarettes were for the priests who taught Latin and studied in Rome during the summer. Cigarettes were for my parents and newscasters and soldiers.

Then came *my* senior year. More than half of the class, but more important most of my friends, had made the smoking decision and wandered up to the hill. The kings of the hill had either gotten early admittance or weren't considering college at all, black and white characters who all smoked Camels. I wanted into this group of rebels. I started bumming cigarettes and standing around with them singing Bob Dylan songs (who had appeared on the cover of *Life* magazine in a Woody Guthrie–style work shirt smoking a Camel) and silently cursing that curious process we were all going through—growing up.

Times passed quickly then. I was college-bound. After three days of orientation, signing papers, and selecting curriculum, and right after my parents' now-empty station wagon pulled out of the parking lot, I walked over to the student union building and bought my first carton. I had arrived. It was official.

In college, cigarettes fit every situation and every person you were with. I'd smoke nonfilters when we'd stay up all night long, filters in the class of the liberal philosophy teacher, who let us smoke while he smoked and taught us the ins and outs of Kierkegaardian thought. Menthols were for the day after and sore throats; Marlboros were available in the cigarette machines in the 3.2 bars, and their crushproof box came in handy at the physical affairs we called dances. We all bummed and borrowed cigarettes from each other and happily smoked our way through college.

In the army, cigarettes were my best friend. The habit was almost encouraged, and everybody from the officers to the lowly privates smoked cigarettes. When the smoking lamp was lit was a strange ritual; policing the area inevitably led to learning how to fieldstrip your butt. Cigarettes were cheap and abundant. Cigarettes and I would stay up at night and dream about civilian life.

I smoked my way through the United States Army and right on into marriage. I was reaching pro status by this time. I had a lighter that I had managed not to lose for about two years, and I had settled on a particular brand; I was actually known for my brand. Camels was the choice: it was exotic, tough (I love the color yellow), and my mother had smoked them—once she told me they always elicited the response, "Oh, you smoke Camels?" People knew and identified me with those Camels, even though I would experiment with other brands. . . .

One year I decided to abandon cigarettes and enrolled in a program designed to rid me of my habit. Our group met in a hotel meeting room after work and was composed of a good slice of society, old, young, big, little, whiny, and quiet, but all of us were office workers from the surrounding area. We, the new "quitters," became more familiar with and identified our smoking traits, the triggers, the Pavlovian responses, the health risks, the evaluation of time . . . it was like one big character-evaluation car wash. Some people dropped out along the way, of course—too much reality, it seemed—but after eight weeks of talking about it, one rainy night, a graduation of sorts took place in that hotel meeting room and six of us had, believe it or not, quit smoking cigarettes.

I couldn't quite believe it, but my life went on without cigarettes. I began nurturing a disdain for smokers that actually grew. It wasn't quite McCarthyesque, because my witch hunts were journeys into habit rather than health. For the first time, I was living my adult life without cigarettes.

But a year or two later . . . I came back. In the middle of Lake Superior not far from where the *Edmund Fitzgerald* had sunk, on a twin-engine Chris-Craft in the most perfect of situations, I reached out and lit a Marlboro for no apparent reason. They were there. Before long I was back in the groove, back to my level and almost unaware that I was even smoking cigarettes again.

I've been there ever since, even though I have vowed to myself to quit when this book is published. I still have a lot of smoking friends, but it tends to annoy everyone a lot more, it's a pain in the ass to have to go out and buy them late at night, in the morning, anytime really, and since the price now is approaching the hundred-dollar mark for cartons, well. . . .

And then there was the big "nonsmoking" hiatus that began for all smokers sometime in the '90s—you couldn't smoke on airplanes suddenly, and the walls for smokers started to close in. It became them and us. Taxation went through the roof, forcing the prices up up up. You had to drive to an Indian reservation fifty miles away to get good prices. Then you couldn't smoke in public places, or bars, and then only in designated areas. There are even outdoor areas in California where you are forbidden to smoke. Hotel rooms, rental cars, restaurants, sports arenas, all boasted of their nonsmoking, or smoke-free, as they say it, status. You have to be a real pro, a dedicated long-ball hitter, to smoke these days, and you smoke with other pros, out in the rain, in front of your favorite tavern on the sidewalk next to the whirring generators.

As a mere product of an electronic, advertising-based, guilt-ridden, image-conscious, money-driven society, I am being constantly questioned or questioning myself about why I smoke cigarettes. The mortality of the situation begs for an answer. The old-fashioned nature (seems so twentieth century), the time consumption (what am I going to do instead, read *TV Guide*?), the smell (factories, locomotives, adulthood all rolled into one), the bother (oh, okay, I'll take an elevator down twenty-five floors and walk half a block to the designated smoking area), the inconsiderateness (move into the other room then), the wasted money, the stains, the burns, and on and on. And in this new world we live in, the libertarian right seems to be the only shield we smokers can conveniently hide behind, the right to be a smoker.

When I put all of these considerations, all the pros, cons (and a few Kools for good measure) into a common blender, I always come up with the same bottom line and answer: I like it.

The author, shortly after he assumed the mantle of smoking only one brand and people began recognizing him for it.

John Rolfe

In 1612, Captain John Rolfe produced the first successful tobacco crop in Virginia. John Rolfe was a farmer in the Jamestown settlement whose crops of tobacco became the economic basis for the colony. Known as an "ardent smoker," Rolfe was probably instrumental in importing tobacco seed from Trinidad between 1610 and 1611. He crossed the imported breed with the indigenous tobacco to produce a plant well adapted to the local soil and reportedly of pleasant taste. When the English cargo vessel *Elizabeth* sailed from Virginia on June 28, 1613, it presumably carried Rolfe's first tobacco crop for export. In April of the following year, John Rolfe married a sweet young Indian named Pocahontas in a Jamestown church. He died early in 1622. Within those ten short years, tobacco became the staple of the colonies, even though the motherland, England, was anxious to have the new provinces produce other commodities, such as flax, cotton, and indigo.

The revenues and profits from the "devil weed," as tobacco had come to be called, changed their minds, though. In 1622, Virginia exported sixty thousand pounds of tobacco from the colonies back to England. Nearly a hundred years later, the production level of export had risen to a whopping 50 million pounds and was still growing.

Rolfe may be considered the father of modern tobacco, through his aggressive sale and distribution of tobacco, but he was also anointed the economic savior of the colonies.

BIC

These tricky little lighters are to smokers what poker chips are to gamblers. According to the company, they now sell about 4 million lighters every day, and that is not bad for a company that started as a ballpoint pen maker. I think over half of these lighters sold today are left on windowsills outside bars, or on cocktail party coffee tables, or inadvertently end up in other people's purses and pockets. Good smokers who go to good smoking gatherings use their lighters like wampum, and they arrive home at times with a rainbow collection of BICs in their possession.

BIC timeline:

1973   The first BIC lighter was released. It featured an adjustable flame.

1985   The BIC Mini was released, and it had a fixed flame size.

1990   The decorative fixed-flame lighter was introduced.

1991   The first BIC electronic lighter was introduced.

1998   The electronic Mini BIC lighter came onto the market.

2005   The BIC Maxi lighter was inducted into the permanent collection of the Museum of Modern Art (MoMA) in New York. It is housed in the Department of Architecture and Design.

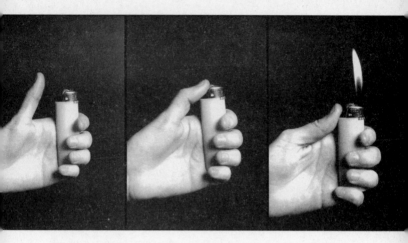

"Flick your BIC," as the saying goes. Basically, utilizing a BIC is a fairly simple process:

Step 1. Position the lighter as shown, with your thumb in the ready position. These lighters are for both right- and left-handed people.

Step 2. Bring your thumb down on the little wheel. The little wheel is attached to a flint somewhere in there that is used to create the spark. The wheel is rotated toward oneself, and at the same time your thumb will naturally move down to a valve that lets the vaporous and highly flammable gas escape from the tube in the lighter.

Step 3. The little BIC creates a flame that will remain ignited as long as you hold the valve down. Besides lighting cigarettes, BICs are great for things like finding your lost car keys in a dark cave or joining the legions of others at a Jerry Garcia tribute, who for some reason ignite their BICs and stare toward the heavens every single time.

> "I love to watch the flame spurt up, love to watch it come closer, filling me with its warmth."
>
> —LUIS BUÑUEL

Three on a Match

The three-on-a-match superstition stems from man's fascination with the mystical number three since early times. Since birth required three people—father, mother, and child—three came to mean life itself.

Early man saw the world around him in terms of three components: He saw himself as body, mind, and spirit; he saw the natural world composed of mineral, vegetable, and animal. The Bible and literature maintained the superstition: Jonah's three exhausting days in the belly of a whale, St. Peter's three denials, and Shakespeare's Macbeth had three witches.

The phrase "three on a match," as legend has it, is derived from early tribal man. When a chieftain died, all tribal fires were extinguished but his. After a period of mourning, the local medicine man relit the tribe's fires, three at a time, with a flame from the dead chieftain's fire, which was believed to contain his spirit. Centuries later this custom was passed on to and adopted by the Christian church.

Soldiers are perhaps the most superstitious about lighting three cigarettes off one match. Supposedly during the First World War, the superstition held that if three soldiers lit their cigarettes from the same match, one of the three would be killed. It has been considered bad luck for three people to share a light from the same match ever since.

The basis for the idea is that it would be night, of course, and when the first soldier lit his cigarette the enemy would see the light; when the second soldier lit his cigarette the enemy would take aim; and when the third soldier lit his cigarette, the enemy would fire.

There was probably no such superstition during the First World War. It has been suggested that the superstition was invented about a decade later by the Swedish match tycoon Ivar Kreuger in an attempt to get people to use more matches, and thus increase his sales.

Weddings are very tricky affairs in the first place and can be jinxed enough, so why would the bride, the groom, and the other fellow—the preacher maybe?—light up, and all together on one match?

Smokers Around
the World

TURKISH OFFICER.

SPANIARD.

S

AUSTRIAN SOLDIER.

BRAZILIAN.

N.

PARISIAN.

ENGLISH NAVAL OFFICER.

BEDOUIN.

PRUSSIAN LIEUTENANT.

15

The Conversation

Cigarettes are great for starting conversations, though "great" is not strong enough a word: they are for cigarette smokers what swords were for the knights of post-Roman western Europe or what pistollas were for the men of Pancho Villa . . . they unite the chosen. In general, smokers like each other and they almost unconsciously use their cigarettes to get them places, to find new people to almost affirm their own existences. We are going to join a conversation at a party now, a party that has been in progress for a while and is beginning to thin. Everyone is a couple of drinks in, and two cigarette smokers find each other. We find "Betty," a lab technician, recently estranged from her boyfriend of five years, meeting "Duke," the owner of a small chain of fast-food Mexican joints.

Betty has pulled out one of her 101 ultra lights and has asked Duke for a light. Duke knows better than to whip out his trusty Zippo, which is snugly put away in his Levi's 501s. Rather, he offers his already burning cigarette as a response to Betty's request.

> Betty: Got a light, dude?
> Duke: The name's Duke . . . here, you can light it off mine.
> Betty: Sure, that's easy enough. Name's Betty.

Betty takes her very sweet time, lingers a bit while she carefully ignites her 101. Duke is careful not to make any physical contact yet, such as holding her wrist steady as she lights up. Besides, they are both holding drinks, and it may seem a little pushy.

> Duke: There you go . . . think you got it, Betty. (He is careful to pronounce her name just as she had stated it seconds earlier.)
> Betty: Ummmm (she mutters as she is inhaling her newly lit cigarette).

Now phase two of the perchance meeting begins. Cigarettes are lit and have been inhaled, and body language is starting to ensue. Betty begins by suggestively rubbing her pinkie finger around the rim of her highball glass, and Duke is emphasizing each of his statements by pointing his cigarette directly at Betty.

> Duke: How do *you* (he points) come to be at *this* (he points again) party?
> Betty: Oh ... (she draws it out for a while, teasingly) I just felt I had to come to Francie's party ... I don't get out much anymore, but like ... Francie is my college roommate and we ... (she very deliberately lets the sentence trail off).

Now the test. Duke is going to test her sense of propriety and sense of humor and see if Betty is willing ... willing to do what? We'll see.

> Duke: Mind if I use your drink as an ashtray? (He says it in a very straightforward, almost lawyerly way.)
> Betty: Oh, go ahead. I can't taste anything at this point anyway. (She is revealing her vulnerability.)

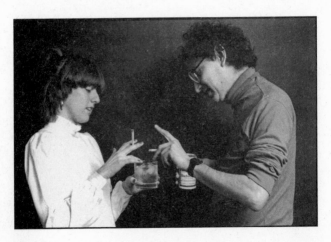

Touché! She is now using his beer can as her ash receptacle. They near each other during this clumsy exercise. Mission accomplished.

Betty: Looks like your beer is almost empty anyway, right?

Duke: (He takes a long drag from his cigarette before answering.) Yeah, but there's plenty more where this one came from, I'm afraid.

The conversation continues, but a new factor has come into the game. Eye contact. Betty is staring right at Duke as Duke decides to shift gears and presents the first fully intimate question of the evening.

Duke: So if you don't get out much anymore, it must mean

you have a boyfriend or . . . something. . . . (His voice trails off with the intention of getting her to respond.)

Betty: Well . . . (She hesitates long enough to make Duke wonder if his declaration is correct.) . . . not at the moment really, er . . . well, there's . . . he's not exactly a *boy*friend, just a friend.

The plot now thickens. Betty now becomes animated and begins wildly gesticulating and fluttering her eyes as she speaks. Duke goes down the opposite road; he's Clark Gable—confident now but passively aggressive as he urges her on.

Duke: So he . . .

Betty: (interrupts him and seemingly begins in mid-sentence) Yeah, I went to Europe, and when I got back, well, we had a talk and I just knew something was up. I just told him to move out, and he like agreed in two seconds. I *was* right! But shit, I had lost him way before that.

Duke: So he moves out and now it's just you, and your new friend comes over once in a while for . . . (He stops and she skillfully cuts him off.)

They are on the same runway now. Both planes are about to take off, and each in their own way hope their destination is the same. Duke takes a long drag, then goes for his beer. Betty closes her eyes slightly as she takes a very long drag.

> Betty: Well, you gotta live, you know. (She flicks her ashes in the opposite direction.) You just can't sit around and . . .
>
> Duke: (Takes a hit on his beer.) You can say that again. You gotta live while you can.

Reality bites. It now suddenly feels like it is getting late, but in fact it has only been two or three minutes. Duke glances at his watch, which means one of two things: he is getting ready to leave, or he is going to suggest a new venue to Betty.

> Betty: Quarter of two, really? Where does the time go at these things? (She waves her arm across the room and it grazes Duke.)
>
> Duke: Time to go? Just kidding. Yeah . . . quarter to two . . . Night's still young!

The next step, the crossroads, the Clash moment. Should I stay or should I go? Time has arrived. Betty seems to be okay with Duke, he seems harmless, maybe a little boring, but not badly built. It's a wait-and-see-what-happens situation as far as she is concerned at this point. Duke's wagon is hitched, he's ready to leave town.

But she's told him she lives right there in the same building, so what is there to lose?

Absolutely nothing, as far as Duke is concerned.

> Betty: Guess I'll finish this cigarette and
> wander home.
> Duke: Yeah, I've been on my fuckin' feet
> all day long. (He inserts the part
> about the arduous day for effect; it
> stresses that he's tough but can see
> things through no matter what.)
> Betty: You could (she skips a beat) rest a
> bit at my place if you want.
> Duke: That's not the worst thing I've
> heard all day. Let's do it.

The deal is complete, the gate is closed and the sun has set. They are leaving together. What better way for cigarette smokers to agree than to symbolically tie the knot by "toasting" with their cigarettes.

> Betty: Shall we? (Her voice has now
> assumed a Betty Boop pitch.)
> Duke: (chuckling) You bet your ashes.

A Special Cigarette Day

A special cigarette day is one in which you rotate a series of different flavors and brands through the course of your waking hours. On this day of days, as a true smoker you're trying to attain that nirvana-like state, you're seeking maximum enjoyment, you're going to enjoy smoking cigarettes to the hilt, you're going to be the real you. Pick a day in the not too distant future and be prepared. Then when the day comes, enjoy.

Here is an example of one smoker's "special" day. Read his notes from the day, learn from them, then create and carve out your own. It is special, and most of all, it's yours.

It is 7:30 a.m. My alarm went off at 7:00. I dawdled for a moment, but now . . . I'm stepping out of the shower and ready to start my special smoking day. A full glass of orange juice awaits me. I decide, why not go for my regular smoke first, my Winston. Start my day as I usually do. So I do. I light it and carry my lit Winston, the orange juice, and an ashtray back to my bedroom and sit them down on the dresser. Whoops, coffee. Gotta make the coffee. That'll be quick, and it requires a quick little cigarette for the task, so how about a nonfilter Camel, I ask myself. Great idea.

Okay, coffee made, I'm back in the bedroom. The Winston has burnt down, so I extinguish that, light another, sip the orange juice, now . . . what to wear? Clothes selected, so now how about some of that coffee. Oh, yes, strong coffee, and I know what goes great with really strong coffee, a Gauloises. Now we're talking. Heavy-duty French stuff. Whip out the old Zippo, light it, and start to feel like a soldier in the Second World War. "Parvelous . . . ?" Think I'll have a couple of these babies, skip the English muffins and stuff.

Time to go. Where is everything? This is going to take a while, better get something extra long, something that will burn a while. How about, hmmm, let's see, a Camel Full Flavor Menthol 100 will do the trick. Get that going, okay now, where's my briefcase, keys, wallet, glasses, what else . . . out the door and into the fresh air. Change of climate and atmosphere, perfect time for a new cigarette. Back to the old reliables, I decide, the Winstons, a couple of them maybe on the way, and hey, who is counting anyway? This is my *special* cigarette day.

Now. Up ahead, there's the office. And I can't smoke in there. It's going to be a while until I can duck out, so what I need now is a cigarette with staying power, something to get me through the next hour or two of no smoking . . . got it, and they always work. Pall Mall. They are long, flavorful, and take a long time to smoke. I get it going. Well, while I'm out here I'll grab a container of coffee, have another Pall Mall—no, make that a Lucky Strike Light, the ones in the box, not the crush-proof ones. Okay, it is nearing ten, time to go in and face the working day.

Round about 11:30 the old gnawing begins, time for a cigarette, and it's going to be in the designated smoking area with the rest of the staff who smoke. I decide to take it easy and go with something that doesn't raise eyebrows, like a Winston Light or an L&M. Since today is my special day, I walk around offering my fellow workers some of my party cigarettes, as I call them. "Here, take it for later. . . ." "Go ahead, try it." "Won't kill ya." I establish myself among my peers, even if I have been smoking with these same people through rain, shine, snow, and thunder for over five years in this dreary designated smoking area.

In we go, time to shuffle some papers and get ready for lunch. I make a lunch date for this special day and make sure my partner is a smoker. I bring a variety of packs with me and mix it up, Rothmans, Merits, American Spirits (just so I can have that conversation about how they, the American Spirits, are really pretty good when it comes right down to it), Kools for some menthol fun, and oh, I throw in a pack of Viceroys just for good measure. I of course offer my lunch date their choice, then I start my heavy rotation routine. Some outdoor cafes allow smoking, all the better if you can find one, and if you do you're a lucky person indeed. After sitting down, I set my platoon of cigarette packages up on the table and expound on each for my guest. "I smoked these in high school," or "My grandfather used to leave these out on his workbench in the garage and as a teenager I would . . ." Cigarette stories are like myth, like age-old sagas handed down from one smoking generation to another, so I spin my wheel and tell my side of the story. I continue smoking through lunch, mixing and matching my brands, volleying smoke rings around the area, fiddling with my lighters. After the bill comes I try to ascertain whether the waiter smokes or not, a fact I could not determine, so I left him a little treat anyway, a fresh pack of Merit Ultra 100s.

Back to the office. This afternoon it is going to be two smoking breaks; it is almost three hours, so why not? I disguise the first one as an errand—the copier needs paper, right, and since I was going that way, why not? I step out and have an old standby,

> **"To me, being grown-up meant smoking cigarettes, drinking cocktails, and dressing up in high heels and glamorous outfits."**
>
> —LORNA LUFT

Lucky Strike. Ah, those tight little Luckies always work. I have a couple, they go quick. My next while-I'm-at-the-office cigarette is going to come about half an hour after what everyone considers a legit break. I amble out to the designated area, greet everyone, not like Caesar coming back into Rome, just a hello or two, and then reach for what I consider the best break cigarette, Dunhill. The original red Dunhills in the box. The ones James Bond smoked. The mere fact I am even smoking Dunhills impresses my fellow workers; they burn slowly, made especially for the long-ball hitters. They are flavorful enough to carry you through to the end of the day. I manage two of them and half a Salem (just to equalize the Dunhill taste) before I go back in.

Workday is done. Now let's get down to business. No more rules, no more "you can't smoke here, you can't smoke there." I can go for the limit now, light them off each other, blow smoke rings, get two or three going just to experience the different draws, the different tastes. Roll a few just for the heck of it. Light 'em with matches, lighters, off the stove, whatever. Smoke and do whatever I want to do is my motto now.

Now I'm headed home. I start by finishing off those dwindling packs of Merits and American Spirits, I still have a way to go. I'm home now, so I go back and dig into my secret cache. I bring out a couple of packs of the generics, the Sandias and Smokin Joes. I keep building my assemblage, brand by brand. Next are my Chesterfields, Belairs, Tareytons, and I might as well finish off those Dunhills. I don't forget my foreign friends either, the Belomorkanals and my gold-tip Russians. This evening from 6:30 p.m. or so until midnight, I make a list as I smoke, the brands, the sensation, the inner feeling, and just keep them going one by one.

Bedtime approaches. Time for my final cigarette of the day. I think long and hard about the day. Which cigarette sticks out in my mind? I smoke that last vaquero for the evening as I sit there by my bedroom window, special. I have that Winston, then have a Camel straight, and think . . . I'm a smoker, and I have just had a helluva day.

Looks like this could be a big drag for these Michigan boys. They each smoked 135 unfiltered cigarettes in five minutes and broke the then-current Guinness World Record achievement. (UPI)

[Note: If you are joining people for drinks after work, stick to something that doesn't raise eyebrows or cause undue conversation. Nonfilters tend to make people think you're a heavy and very serious smoker. Lights imply that you are a wimp or just experimenting. Go with your typical Marlboro Reds in a box, your Winstons, and enjoy the liberty, enjoy the company and the smoke.]

Moderate Smoker

Paramount Studios was the first of the motion-picture studios to adopt a cigarette coupon program for all of its employees. The program itself was designed for both the lowly messenger girls and the lurid blondes who achieved the status of "movie star." It entitled them to a fresh package of cigarettes every week. The honor system was strictly observed.

As a moderate smoker, you might want to consider getting out of the little league or the under-forty-a-day group and stepping up to the elite class, commonly referred to as the "heavy" smoker. Here are a few handy suggestions for increasing your daily consumption.

As a general rule, mealtimes are reserved for consumption of food and drink. But, smoking during the course of a meal is not only an excellent way to step up your daily habit, it's an excellent way as well of mixing conversation, good food and drink, and, of course, smoke.

Begin your new smoking-and-eating ritual by slowing down your present habit of large bites of food followed by huge swallows or pulls on your beverage. What's the rush now? Formerly, your philosophy was to rush through the meal in order to get to that all-important after-the-meal smoke. Now the two rituals are one!

The first thing to change is your routine. Bring your cigarettes to the table along with a large ashtray and plenty of matches, lighters, whatever. Light up before you sit down and keep one going at all times. After small sips of your beverage, follow with at least three or four deep drags on your cigarette. Follow the same steps with food. Eat and smoke slowly and deliberately. Punctuate each course with three or four cigarettes. With your coffee and after-dinner drink, to be cordial and a little old style, offer cigarettes to the others around the table.

With practice, you will easily be able to increase your daily habit. At the average meal you may be able to attain the pack-a-meal plateau, but it will take courage and, most important, practice. Expect to spend far more time at each meal. In the future, you will avoid the "smoker's rush" and you will gain weight, but, most important, your smoker's status will have shifted from that of the casual "Oh, I'm about a pack-a-day" smoker to that of the "heavy" smoker.

Did You Know?

The mid-1950s saw the large emergence of menthol cigarettes. Of the five introduced within a two-and-a-half-year period, three of them, Oasis, Newport, and Spud, also featured an innovation in cigarette packaging: flip-top boxes.

Cat Tyc Profile

MY NAME
Catherine Tyc

CHILDHOOD DREAM
I always wanted to be a writer. I think I wanted to be a fireman once, too. And Princess Di after watching her wedding on TV. And an MTV VJ.

FONDEST MEMORY
This is sort of a bittersweet memory, but my fondest memory is swimming in a pool with an old love. This person didn't let me go and I felt such trust that eventually my fear left me for a second and I did float, so it's bittersweet because that person is long gone, but I am fond of that memory because at least I know that a certain elevated level of trust in people is possible. I guess this is a metaphor of sorts for transcending fear.

SOUNDTRACK
The Whitey Album by Ciccone Youth

RETREAT
The Shakespearean theater behind my mom's house in Stratford, Connecticut. Or a weeping willow tree behind the theater.

WILDEST DREAM
Being the first woman to win the Academy Award for Best Director

PROUDEST MOMENT
My first video screening at the Brooklyn Museum of Art.

BIGGEST CHALLENGE
Directing a cast and crew to make a music video in my basement.

PERFECT DAY
Rain. No appointments. No place to be. Tea. Books. And a stack of DVDs. A refrigerator full of food and a cat purring on my lap.

FIRST JOB
I was a summer nanny when I was fourteen and then I worked in my town video store until my senior year of high school.

INDULGENCE
Handbags. Sushi. Chocolate. Coffee.

FAVORITE MOVIE
This is a hard question to answer. *Wings of Desire* by Wim Wenders or *No Such Thing* by Hal Hartley.

INSPIRATION
Poetry, Bill Viola, DIY-ness, Mary J. Blige, punk rock, to rip a quote from my friend's Friendster profile, "feminism, disappointment and sarcasm."

MY LIFE
Do you mean what I do with my time? This is what takes up my time: tutor helpline assistant for Oregon Literacy, art school student, writing, video art, editing for Chiasmus Press, curator of video art series, karaoke singer.

MY CIGARETTE
Parliament Lights.

31

"If alcohol is queen, then tobacco is her consort. It's a fond companion for all occasions, a loyal friend through fair weather and foul. People smoke to celebrate a happy moment, or to hide a bitter regret. Whether you're alone or with friends, it's a joy for all the senses. What lovelier sight is there than that double row of white cigarettes, lined up like soldiers on parade and wrapped in silver paper?"

—Luis Buñuel

Did You Know?

L&M was the favorite brand of First Lady Jacqueline Kennedy; however, she saw the Liggett & Myers presidential cigarettes as a form of advertising and believed that they cheapened the presidency. Nevertheless, the First Lady smoked these special L&Ms, and two of her authenticated empty packs were auctioned off last year, selling for about $200 each.

Billboards

Not strictly a billboard for cigarettes, but for Mail Pouch chewing tobacco, this is probably the most notorious tobacco billboard advertisement in the United States. (Photograph courtesy of Elmer Napier of Vienna, West Virginia)

On April 22, 1999, the last cigarette billboard in the United States was gone, marking a colorful era that had begun in the nineteenth century. The cigarette billboards had a marvelous run for about a hundred years. Highlights include a Chesterfield sign in Atlantic City on the Steeplechase Pier, designed and built by the R. C. Maxwell Company of Trenton, that was illuminated with thirteen thousand lightbulbs. Every seventy-five seconds the entire display would go through a twenty-seven-step cycle illuminating the colored bulbs before starting again. Times Square had a Camel sign, a spectacular they dubbed it, that had the face of a very happy smoker blowing out four-foot piston-driven smoke rings made from steam above the bustling New Yorkers below.

The new golden age of cigarette billboard advertising was initiated in the 1980s, when one out of every three billboards featured a tobacco product. A government act passed in 1971 banned cigarette ads on both television and radio, thus setting the stage for the billboard era. The death of cigarette billboards, as noted above, was April 22, which is coincidentally two things: Earth Day and the day Henry VIII ascended the throne in England in 1509, which has nothing to do with this book, but since. . . . But once again it is interesting to note how cigarettes and the advertising world were always working hand in hand.

An art lover examines the Pop Art of Tom Wesselman's *Smoker, 1 (Mouth 12)* on display at the Tel Aviv Museum of Art. (UPI)

"Dig deep," as they say. This gentleman is not only going to
pay dearly for his cigarettes, but is also going to be fined fairly
heavily for smoking in a supermarket as well, if he is caught.
Laws passed in the state of California in 1975 prohibited
smoking in supermarkets (which used to be a lot of fun),
theaters, public restrooms, and on public transportation.
Other taboo places were soon to follow.

Buying Cigarettes

Buying cigarettes is an art in itself. And no two smokers do it the same way. One can buy them casually, pack by pack, or he may be a tag-along type: "Oh, honey, if you are going to the store, could you pick me up a pack of Doral 100s." And then there are multi-pack buyers, Internet purchasers, phone orderers, the list goes on. So for the moment, let us consider perhaps one of the most important and in many ways the most gratifying rituals in the whole cigarette smoking process: buying cigarettes.

Basically, there are four ways to buy. First is the over-the-counter, one-pack-at-a-time method from everywhere from supermarkets, gas stations (some still carry them in the little glass cases by the cash register; most of them these days have these space-age marts sewn next to them that carry cigarettes) to delicatessens, newsstands, and occasionally pharmacies. Second is to buy them in cartons, and cartons can be bought in basically the same locales as single packs, but they are more expensive that way unless you go to an Indian reservation or a tax-free store in an international airport. Third is the newest option and the one under the most scrutiny because you avoid all taxation: the Internet. Loads of brands and exotic flavors there. And fourth is buying them off friends or people on the street as "Lucys" or "Looseys," this being the hardest and most humiliating way because you usually don't get the brand you want and the people look at you like, "What is this guy, a cheapskate or down on his luck or worse?" but you can come back with, "I'm trying to quit and don't want to buy any packs." . . . Usually does the trick.

In an over-the-counter purchase there are two players, you and someone behind a counter who is standing near a cash register. You are the buyer; they are the seller. Behind the seller or in the vicinity there will be a cigarette rack with all the different brands to be sold. They are usually sorted by brand. These are high-traffic areas, meaning lots of customers come and go, so there is little or no room for lingering or deciding. Most counter personnel will demand a quick response. And they don't recommend or try to persuade you with something like "Why not a good old pack of Pall Malls?" The best thing is to have your mind made up before stepping to the counter. Be frank, unashamed, be proud, and be exact. With over twenty-four varieties of Camels, you have to say, "Two fresh packs of Camel Light Menthol Box Kings, please," and not just "Camels." And have your money ready. No one in this game likes to stand and wait for someone to fish through their pockets or purse for loose coins or bills, and then after all of that change their minds. This is a quick and speedy swap. If you want matches, ask for them then, not later. If you are to get change, you'll get it momentarily. Grab it and your smokes, then exit. End of story, you are on your way.

Cigarette machine (what few there are left) prices in general are slightly higher than over-the-counter, carton, and Internet buys. These machines are usually found in down-market gas stations, bus and train depots, and bowling alleys, but in general they are on the wane because the government thinks kids will gravitate toward them and spend all their hard-earned money on cigarettes instead of staying home and reading the classics with their parents. There are a few other downsides to buying from machines: there is less variety available; the cigarettes themselves can become pretty stale, some of them having sat there since 1974; and, finally, many, perhaps all, machines don't supply matches. Where you will not find cigarette machines is hospitals, national parks, day care centers, churches and synagogues, or elevators, so don't look and don't ask.

This is one of the famous Chesterfield Girls from the early 1940s. She has a lot of things going for her here: the Hornblower hat, the epaulets, the wavy blonde hair, and, of course, the cigarettes in the spyglass.

If you can find a cigarette machine, there are two types, the non-bending electric button ones and the bending lever ones. The lever machine usually requires exact change (and that is a lot of fun when you have to go find eight or nine dollars in quarters); the button ones will give you change, sometimes. Some have matches buttons, but not many. The wisdom here is to avoid machines except in the darkest of moments, and every smoker knows when those are.

The most economical and sensible and perhaps the most enjoyable method is carton or case buying. These purchases can be made at big supermarkets, at Indian reservations, and of course over the Internet. In the case of the supermarket, select two or three cartons and hide them among your other groceries if your family is giving you trouble. Writing to the tobacco companies for twenty-five cartons or more used to be a breeze, but the companies are not doing that as readily as before, with all the news and reports of black-market cigarettes. So that leaves you the Indian reservations, and if your home or office is near one they can be handy and inexpensive and they are not that intense. Many have drive-by windows; it can be pretty intense, but you simply follow the arrows. Their selections are usually pretty good. So be brave and don't have reservations about buying from the Indians.

> **"I sometimes look at myself, I'm sitting with a biro and cigarette packet, desperately scrawling dribble on it. And sometimes, I put down my fag pack and think, what am I, a grown man, doing at this hour of the night? Then I banish that thought, pick the fag pack up again."**
>
> —JOE STRUMMER

The Internet created a virtual tsunami in the cigarette world. Suddenly you could order by the truckload and not be questioned. And the cigarettes sold, came from Switzerland but were American brands, go figure. But now in the privacy of your own home or office, or the summer cabin or your in-laws trailer . . . what I am trying to say here is wherever you have Internet access you can fly off to the world of cigarettes in a move of the mouse. And the site names—cigarettesexpress.com, cigarettesforless.com, discountcheapcigarettes.com— are very twenty-first-century in-your-face names. Most premium brands are available and are delivered fresh to your doorstep within an average of ten to twenty-five working days.

There is something strangely un-American about the whole Internet thing. I share with you some copy from one of the sites; www.cigsforless-sale.com offers to you a wide variety of cigarettes for actually low prices: *We able to present you such opportunity owing to the direct export of cigarettes from manufacturers. Due to that we assure not only low prices but also fresh tobacco products for you to taste and enjoy.*

Having read this you now have the most essential information in the whole smoking process: you know where to get them.

Did You Know?

In 1998, the actress Gwyneth Paltrow admitted her love of the cigarette: "I smoke. I smoke Camel Lights. I'm not going to stop."

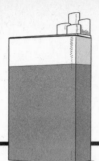

American Spirit Profile

A certain goodness just radiates like a southwestern sunset from the American Spirit smokers. They are just so American, so natural, and so confident in their ways. They go to movies that they discuss them afterward in bars that have sawdust on the floor, they study the L.L.Bean catalogue very closely for the clothes that they wear in Maine as they drink Poland Spring and check their BlackBerrys. Their music is vintage rock, there is little or no hard liquor in their pantries, and they feel that the war in the Middle East is something they just have to accept, like the Visa bill they pay every month.

MALE NAMES
Eric, Jonah, David, Dylan, Joshua, Mikah

FEMALE NAMES
Jessie, Maya, Prudence, Melanie, Rhiann

OCCUPATIONS
Teach for America Fellow, Greenpeace volunteer, wine store employee, vintage furniture salesman, and tropical fish wholesaler

AGE RANGE
22–70

AWARDS AND PRIZES

Completion of five punch cards at a Fair Trade coffee emporium, L.L.Bean shopping sweepstake finalist (prize: two pairs of Eucalyptus Classic Chinos and a hooded Cranberry fleece), competitor in the Apple Cider Century Bicycle Tour in Michigan, five-year safety driving award from Geico

RELIGION

Buddhism and nonsectarian

EDUCATION

BA and night-school brushup courses at the local junior college. Completes the *Los Angeles Times* Sunday magazine crossword puzzle about once every five to six weeks.

LAST BOOK READ

Siddartha by Herman Hesse

Camel Questions Game

The old game of "Camel Questions" can be fun as well as a way to wile away the hours as you sit out in the car smoking and waiting for a family member who is in the Piggly Wiggly shopping for groceries. Take out a couple of packs of Camels—a pack of nonfilters and a pack of filters—to answer some of the questions. True aficionados of the Burley blend will have no problem with the following:

1. How many *E*s are there in the little paragraph above the line on the back of the package?
2. How many camels are there in a pack of Camels?
3. What was the name of the original camel that was photographed for the original pack design?
4. If you were out in the middle of the desert, like the scene depicted on the front panel of the Camel package, where would you stay, under the pyramid, under the palm trees, or under the camel?
5. Where is the lion on the camel?
6. How many doctors out of three smoked Camels during the 1950s?

7. What tobacco company originally produced Camels and in what year?

8. Why does the cost of the tobaccos blended in Camel cigarettes prohibit the use of premiums or coupons?

9. What did the T in the T-Zone (an advertising vehicle in the 1940s and 1950s) stand for?

10. How many Camels can you fit through the eye of a needle?

11. Name five famous people who have endorsed Camels.

12. True or false? The dromedary (Arabian camel) is used as the brand's logo.

This book purposely does not supply the answers to these questions. They are supposed to be provocative and make you think. And make you smoke with a clearer understanding of the product—that is, if you are a Camel smoker.

> **"**Smoking cigarettes seems to alarm peace activists much more than voting for Reagan does.**"**
>
> —P. J. O'Rourke

45

Catherine Zeta-Jones

The ultra-stunning actress Catherine Zeta-Jones arrives at the premiere of Columbia Pictures' *The Legend of Zorro* at the Orpheum Theater on October 16, 2005, in Los Angeles, California. (Photo by Kevin Winter/Getty Images)

"Everybody smokes! Models, actresses, everyone! Don't they realize that it's gross? I understand it's an addiction, but it still pains me to see my friends do it."

—KIRSTEN DUNST

In November of 2005, it was reported by the *Daily Mail* of London that Catherine Zeta-Jones flew in her own airplane not only because of the convenience and luxury of it all but because she could smoke cigarettes. Her husband smokes cigarettes, so it makes logical sense. It is rumored that Catherine is a very very nervous flier and cigarettes tend to calm her down. But while she was doing all the traveling and the hard work on her film *Zorro* she lost her voice. Let's call it a stress-related loss.

Now let's put this hiding away in jet planes to smoke in another context. In May of 2005, two British magazines, *Hello* and *OK!*, were engaged in big court battles about the exclusivity and the right to photograph the infamous Zeta-Jones–Douglas wedding. May we, in a cultural context, insert a little conjecture here? Was it an all-smoking wedding? Were the "I dos" whispered after exhaling a lung full of fresh Marlboro smoke? Was that the brouhaha? Was it not the wish of our Welsh beauty and Hollywood strongman to be photographed flicking ashes and teasing each other with their BICs? We will never ever really know. For the record, it could have been one of the most famous smoking weddings of all time.

Did You Know?

During the First World War, a daring General John J. Pershing, when asked his requirements for victory, replied, "You ask me what we need to win this war. I answer tobacco as much as bullets."

Christmas

Way back in the '40s and '50s, when smoking was perfectly acceptable, cigarettes and the holidays went hand in hand. The cigarette companies created special packaging just for the season. They were the perfect gift, the stocking stuffer as far as the family was concerned, and they served their purpose for the clients, service people, and casual friends in your life. Chesterfield advertisements of the time featured the prototypical Coca-Cola Santa going down snowy chimneys across the land with a bag full of cartons, adorning and decorating the Christmas trees with single packs of Chesterfields and flying away in his reindeer-driven sled with the entire portmanteau filled with cigarettes. Smokers were encouraged to exchange cigarettes at Christmas. They went skiing, drank eggnog, and opened their gifts with cigarettes in their hands. Christmas was so much better then.

Today it is filled with $1,500 flocked Christmas trees, holly imported from Scotland, multicolored poinsettias, mistletoe belt buckles, swags, wreaths shipped to your door direct from the mistletoe.com warehouses, Santa Claus with an electronic attitude, Nativity scenes that include 50 Cent, angels in Victoria's Secret seconds, carolers, nutcrackers, toy soldiers that double as nutcrackers, sleighs, sleds with built in iPods, drums, drummer boys, bows, reindeer and mail-order reindeer meat (diced or filleted), micro-battery-powered Christmas tree ornaments, gingerbread people and gingerbread houses from all parts of the world, Willy Wonka mango melon variety candies, stars, snowflakes, snowmen, and penguins, but alas, cigarettes have been phased out of the Christmas cycle of gift giving.

Infamous Cigarette Smokers

A young **Liza Minnelli** being made up and taking a cigarette break from her title role in the film *Tell Me That You Love Me, Junie Moon*. (UPI)

Brooke Shields after growing out of her *Pretty Baby* stage. This particular ad was created by the Department of Health and Human Services and was scrapped without ever being run. *The Advocate* stated in 2000, "The girl with the cigarettes coming out of her ears, the most celebrated virgin—she must have gone to her publicist and said, 'I want to smoke, I want to take off all my clothes, and I want to be gay.' But when someone sets out just to change their image like that, it's contrived."

The author **Colleen McCullough** fielding questions from the press on her controversial bestseller *The Thorn Birds*.

Pablo Picasso, firing up a Gauloises. Cigarettes didn't cramp his style; he went on to live to about age ninety-two. Picasso produced about 13,500 paintings or designs, 100,000 prints or engravings, 34,000 book illustrations, and 300 sculptures or ceramics. One celebratory cigarette after completing each of those adds up.

Dean Martin seemed to always have a cigarette in hand. Joking around onstage with Jerry Lewis, on the set of *Rio Bravo*, running in the alleys of Vegas with the Rat Pack in a clean white shirt, he always had one going in his right hand. But they caught up with him, and as Santa Claus was coming down the chimney on Christmas Day '95, Dino sighed his last "Amore."

The actresses **Karen Black** and **Cher** share a private moment, gossiping perhaps about their costar in *Come Back to the Five and Dime, Jimmy Dean, Jimmy Dean,* Sandy Dennis.

The thinking Beatle, **John Lennon** was devoted to his cigarettes during his self-imposed exile in the Dakota apartment house in New York during the 1970s.

The guitarist **Keith Richards** of the Rolling Stones, the coconut tree climber, lounges in his New York office during a 1980 portrait session. (Photo by George Rose/ Getty Images)

Potty-mouthed singer **Courtney Love** smoking onstage during the Comedy Central Roast of the ever-talented Pamela Anderson at Sony Studios in August 2005. (Photo by Frank Micelotta/Getty Images)

The singer/guitarist **Kurt Cobain** takes a smoke break while performing with his rough-hewn, flannel-shirted group Nirvana at a taping of the television program *MTV Unplugged*, in November 1993. (Photo by Frank Micelotta/Getty Images)

The actor **Philip Seymour Hoffman** smokes a cigarette during the photocall of the movie *Capote*, presented in competition at the 56th Berlin Film Festival in February 2006. (Johannes Eisele/AFP/Getty Images)

Way back when actors could and would appear in ads for cigarettes, **Bob Hope**, portrayed here, not only smoked Chesterfields in real life but actually became a paid spokesperson for Chesterfield.

The English singer, musician, and actor, the guy who can do it all, **David Bowie**, sporting dyed red hair à la Woody Woodpecker and a yellow zoot suit. Looking just too cool for school in the early 1970s. (Photo by Terry O'Neill/Hulton Archive/ Getty Images)

With her Greta Garbo–like sunglasses, **Princess Margaret**, a heavy smoker in her heyday, watches the Wimbledon tennis matches in the mid 1960s. (UPI/ CablePhoto)

Rudyard Kipling, like many of his generation, never let a huge mustache get in the way of a good smoke. (Library of Congress)

Enrico Caruso, one of the most famous tenors in the history of opera, smoked up to sixty cigarettes a day and was convinced that he could protect his health by keeping a dried anchovy suspended over his chest, hanging from a necklace. He died of bronchial pneumonia at the age of forty-eight.

Slash, appearing on The *Tonight Show with Jay Leno* with his band, Velvet Revolver, in October 2004, in Burbank, California. The cigarette "banning" laws were already in place in California at this time, so how did Slash get away with it? Just goes to show that the law does not apply to everybody. (Kevin Winter/ Getty Images)

Cigarette Pack

What is commonly called a pack of cigarettes is as follows:

The package itself is a paper-made rectangular container measuring approximately 3¼" x 2¼" x 1". There are cigarettes stored inside this container in a flavor-protective foil that usually varies in color and texture according to the encased brand of cigarettes. Gold and silver are the most common colors. The whole package is sealed by transparent, airtight cellophane.

This cellophane wrapping uses a pull-tab system, a thin, ⅛", usually red strip that encompasses the package at either the top (this would be for soft packs, which are made of fairly thin paper and are not reclosable) or about an inch down near the lid hinge (for hard packs, which are composed of sturdy cardboard that creates the "box" effect and are reclosable). By pulling this red tab or strip in a clockwise motion, the package is opened.

The packages are uniformly the same width; this at one time was to accommodate the cigarette machines. They vary in height (that would be the 3¼" dimension) to accommodate the different lengths that cigarettes come in—Kings, 100 millimeter, and your shorty non-filters. Regardless of the length, the packages do fit very well into the breast pocket of most shirts, both male and female, and are easily stored in purses, attaché cases, backpacks, and so forth.

Twenty cigarettes per package is the standard in the United States. In Europe, however, the number of cigarettes per pack can change; taxes, and thus the price of smokes, are constantly fluctuating, but Europeans like to maintain the same price for a pack of smokes, regardless of how many are in the package.

I have often wondered, why this twenty? The average person sleeps, let's say, eight hours a night. And for the most part, you can't smoke while you sleep. This leaves one awake sixteen hours a day. Sixteen hours to smoke. That averages out to be about one cigarette an hour, and throw a couple in for good measure for those extra cups of coffee or "that's not my phone ringing again!" moments, and it comes out to twenty or—a pack a day. How many smokers sitting shirtless up on the paper-covered examination table at their doctor's office answer the inevitable smoking question with, "Oh, you know, Doc . . . about a pack a day, a little less, usually."

Did You Know?

An advertisement in *Life* magazine in 1915 offered the personalized service of initialing each cigarette with your own monogram if you ordered five hundred cigarettes or more.

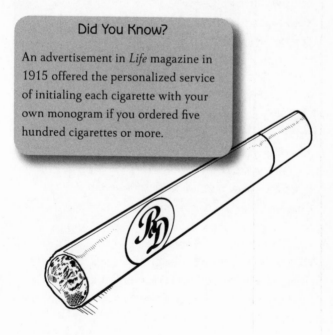

Elders

Golda Meir, the "Iron Lady," served as the prime minister of Israel for five years and is pictured here smoking away at the age of seventy-two. One wonders if the current smoking rules would have been imposed in Israel during her reign. (UPI photo)

When your elders start exhibiting those husky phlegmy coughs early in the morning, the ones that drive the pets howling into the yard and children back into their rooms to play "Look for Barney" on the Internet, it's probably time to suggest a modified cigarette smoking program to them.

The first step is a change of brands. Instead of having one of their favorite 85-millimeter nonfilters continuously burning in their yellowing fingers, suggest that they try a modern-age multifilter light in a gaily adorned package.

Next, have them choose their new cigarettes for the day and have them stick to those only. Develop a program for them. Suggestions for smoking times could be: after their morning movement, before watching *General Hospital*, out at the mailbox after their half-hour trek to retrieve the bills, after their afternoon nap, and prior to the evening cocktail that will usher them into a state of nirvana—and that one would be the final one of the day.

> **"The believing we do something when we do nothing is the first illusion of tobacco."**
> —RALPH WALDO EMERSON

When they start their new program, take the cigarette triggers away: that second cup of their heavily creamed and sugared coffee, the Alpha Kappa Psi ashtray from college, Uncle Waddie's Zippo from Omaha Beach, anything that reminds them of cigarettes. Now help them manage their time a little better and away from cigarettes. Suggestions include: keeping them in the shower or bathtub for long periods of time, consuming their free time by making them wait in the car ("I'll be right out, Mother ..."), church or synagogue attendance, going through stacks of travel brochures ("I think you and Dad would love a three-week cruise in the Adriatic"), large-type Sudoku, and so forth. Busy hands and busy minds keep them out of the devil's workshop. Be creative. Pat them on the back (not too hard) if they succeed; don't ridicule or make a point of ridiculing them in public places if they don't succeed.

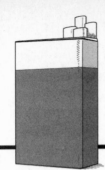

Benson & Hedges Profile

Benson & Hedges smokers are the thinkers in our society, the queen bees, the people with more money in checking than the common man's 401(k) plan. They started wearing glasses when they were still in grade school, hung around the library instead of the playing fields, were altar boys or choir singers, or precociously succeeded in building a salt-based volcano for the science fair without their parents' help. As adults, they maintain and pay all of their monthly bills on time, and they polish their digital camera lenses before leaving for vacation at some well-appointed English-speaking island in the Caribbean. They prefer hot Earl Grey tea to coffee and drive BMWs (station cars) with GPS systems and sheepskins on the front seat.

MALE NAMES
Alvin, Arthur, Dennis, Karl, Justin

FEMALE NAMES
Loretta, Mildred, Evelyn, Christina

OCCUPATIONS
part-time reference librarian, epidemiological nurse, financial aid counselor, hedge fund underwriter, paralegal (while attending school), mechanical waste surveyor

AGE RANGE
45–60

AWARDS AND PRIZES

Artnews essay finalist, 1450 combined SAT scores, Applied Probability Society applicant, Maine State Lottery ticket, internship at the Naval Historical Center in Annapolis, Maryland

RELIGION

Christian Science

EDUCATION

college, graduate, and some Ph.D.s

SALARY RANGE

$350,000-plus

LAST BOOK READ

Rich Dad, Poor Dad by Robert T. Kiyosaki

End of the Ritual

Putting out a cigarette is as important a function as lighting a cigarette. It's all part of the ritual. It's the end of the day. The folding of the tent. The circus has left town. Elvis has left the building.

Careless smokers, neophytes, or "light" smokers will at times be guilty of not extinguishing their cigarettes fully in a partially filled ashtray. The unextinguished, smoldering cigarette butt tends to set other butts afire until the whole ashtray sends up a factory-like filtery after-smell. At parties with festering ashtrays, nonsmokers tend to back off into corners or step into the yard, and their regard for the host of the party is permanently changed.

The most common way of extinguishing a cigarette is to break or snap it, as the photo shows. Crush it out altogether until no more smoke appears. No smoke, fire is out.

When using an ashtray with a prominent edge, flick the burning ash off the butt, then extinguish the glowing ember by crushing it with the remaining part of the cigarette.

Other methods include running your glowing cigarette under a tap until you hear the sizzle, then tossing it in a waste receptacle; dropping it in the toilet, of course; and, last but not least, the shoe routine, where the burning butt is thrown onto a level surface then stepped on. One may either continue to stand on the butt or move their foot in a back-and-forth motion to get the same result.

Did You Know?

During the Vietnam War, cigarette manufacturers sent order blanks for tax-free shipments (usually in fifty-pack increments) to soldiers in the field. After their selections were made, and the shipments were paid for, factory-fresh cigarettes would be delivered within a matter of days to the ordering soldiers at their specific battle sites.

Peter Pavia Profile

MY NAME
Peter Pavia

CHILDHOOD DREAM
My childhood dream was to be a comic book artist, maybe a cartoonist. Unfortunately, subtlety of line eluded me. I could barely draw straight ones.

FONDEST MEMORY
Has to be the evening my daughter Teresa was born. I wandered the Washington Heights neighborhood near Columbia Presbyterian Hospital excitedly phoning relatives. I found a Dominican restaurant that was doing take-out and brought some plantains, rice and beans, and a batida back to the new mother.

SOUNDTRACK
A high, lonesome sound.

RETREAT
One day I hope to be able to afford one.

WILDEST DREAM
My wildest dream masquerades as a death wish. I do my best to avoid it.

PROUDEST MOMENT
Memorial Day 2004. I sold my first novel, a tattered manuscript pounded out on a Royal typewriter. It had languished at the bottom of a closet for five years. A guy

named Charles Ardai had the actual balls to publish the thing, *Dutch Uncle*.

BIGGEST CHALLENGE
To keep hope alive.

PERFECT DAY
Would begin on an early morning in the month of October. I'd run under a bright azure sky and cover more distance than I ever have previously. I would then negate any health benefits I hoped to gain from such healthful activity with a steak, eggs, and pancakes breakfast. After completing a solid morning's worth of writing (ideally, something in a late-stage draft), I'd catch up with my friends in the afternoon and meet my wife for a rare date. Maybe dinner and the theater. I'm a boring grinder who aspires to nothing more than a middle-class existence. Okay, maybe upper-middle-class.

FIRST JOB
Stock boy at the WAB drugstore I had previously shoplifted from. They must have forgotten.

INDULGENCE
Watching maybe a hundred baseball games per season, from first pitch to last?

FAVORITE MOVIE
Tough call. Hard to have one favorite. Early Scorsese pictures are nearest to my sensibility, but *The Friends of Eddie Coyle* is the kind of movie I'd like to make if I had the chance. Most recently, *L.A. Confidential*. But it's not all guns and gangsters. I like a good kid movie, too. *Pinocchio*. And *Mary Poppins* is practically perfect in every way.

INSPIRATION
Anybody who is unapologetic about who they are and what they do, from corrupt politicians (although their

tearful apologies now blight the landscape) to cloistered monks. I would have said Iggy Pop at one point in my life, but I don't have any heroes.

MY LIFE
Continues to improve.

MY CIGARETTE
Camel regular. Straight. No filter. The small ones. I usually have to rehearse all that before I actually buy them, to overcome the cashier's incredulity that an actual live human being is still smoking them.

Did You Know?

LONDON (August 21, 2006)—Turner Broadcasting is scouring more than 1,500 classic Hanna-Barbera cartoons, including old favorites *Tom and Jerry*, *The Flintstones*, and *Scooby-Doo*, to edit out scenes that glamorize smoking. *AOL Entertainment News*

Fieldstripping

Discarded cigarette butts and matches. They may not seem like significant military factors at first glance, and on an urban battlefield they ordinarily wouldn't be. But try sneaking through a remote forest with an experienced guerrilla on your trail, and that one dropped butt may be the clue that leads the enemy to his prey—you!

Fieldstripping a smoke is a soldier's first lesson in cleanliness in the field. For the most part, nonfilter cigarettes when flicked into a clean dry area with ventilation will burn themselves out. Filter cigarettes pose another problem. The chemical filters don't burn. So study the illustrations and follow the step-by-step procedure for proper disposal.

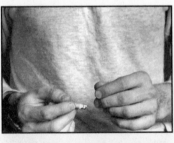

Grab your cigarette and prepare to get rid of the burning ash.

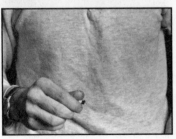

By rotating the cigarette back and forth you can make the ash fall off or out.

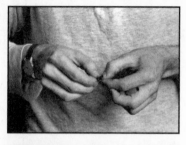

With the ash now gone, separate the rest of the tobacco from the butt.

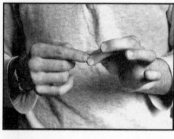

Wad the remaining paper and butt into a ball.

Ready for disposal!

This quiz will help you discover if you have a cigarette litter awareness problem.

1. The long stretches of sandy areas adjacent to large bodies of water are generally known as
   A. beaches.
   B. giant coastal ashtrays.
2. Cigarette butts are biodegradable.
   A. True—they are made of magic material that turns into dirt, sand, or brick depending on where you drop them.
   B. False—they are made of plastic fibers that take many years to decompose.
3. The best place to dispose of a cigarette is
   A. a public ashtray, car ashtray, disposable

ashtray, or a standard trash can after field-stripping.

    B. wherever you happen to be the exact moment you are finished with it.

4. Cigarette butts contain toxic chemicals that leak out into the environment.

    A. True—the filter is specifically designed to trap these chemicals.

    B. False—the filters are nontoxic and nutritious for the infants and animals that may swallow them.

5. Cigarette butts make the perfect gardening mulch.

    A. True—the unnatural colors lend contrast to the cedar mulch in public gardens.

    B. False—cigarette butts turn public gardens into public ashtrays.

6. Standing on the edge of the Grand Canyon or other natural wonder, your first reaction is

    A. what incredible beauty!

    B. what a great place to flick my butt!

7. The spaces between sidewalk bricks and concrete slabs are designed to

    A. allow the materials to expand and contract in hot and cold weather without cracking.

    B. catch littered cigarette butts and display them for pedestrian viewing.

8. Littered cigarette butts cause numerous fires every year.

    A. True—not all fires are caused by cigarette butts, but many are.

    B. False—the idea that a burning cigarette flicked into dry timber could spark a fire is ludicrous!

9. How many cigarettes are estimated to be littered each year worldwide?

    A. Several trillion. Assuming the 1.3 billion smokers litter an average of five butts a day.

B. Not many. I only litter about five a day myself.

10. The best thing to do with cigarette butts on a nature trail is

    A. hang on to them and throw them out later, just like other trash.

    B. flick them periodically on the trail to mark your way back and avoid getting lost.

ANSWERS

If you actually need the answers then you probably didn't pass.

Did You Know?

In 1937, the Brown & Williamson Tobacco Corporation sent a huge sound truck, complete with broadcasting and amplifying equipment, motion-picture screens, and projectors on a nationwide tour covering twenty-five states to publicize Kool and

Forbidden Places

Places where smoking is forbidden have always been a nuisance to a good cigarette smoker. A good cigarette smoker wants to smoke everywhere, at any time, and enjoy life.

We always see No Smoking signs, and more and more these days, almost to the point of redundancy. My question is: Why don't we ever see Please Smoke signs? I can think of lots of good places where they would work. But just as a reminder so you don't commit the ultimate cultural faux pas, here's a list of the ultra-taboo areas.

1. Hospital elevators
2. Churches and synagogues, places of worship in general
3. Nursery schools for the mentally challenged
4. Airplane lavatories (on both domestic and inter national flights)
5. Caves associated with the National Park System
6. During solemn wedding ceremonies held inside
7. Movie houses, theaters, playhouses
8. Train dining cars
9. Infirmaries with oxygen tanks
10. Subways, buses, and most public transportation
11. Gas stations (including those that offer diesel fuel)
12. Courts of law
13. Toddler sections in department stores
14. Supermarkets with teeming fruit and vegetable bins
15. Glassed-in botanical gardens
16. Indoor sports arenas
17. Public libraries, bookstores
18. Museums featuring art from the Renaissance
19. Butterfly emporiums or conservatories

"This is satisfaction—*man-size* satisfaction! Chesterfield."

—FRANK SINATRA

What is wrong with this picture? First, the guy may be smoking where flammable fumes could come up out of the sewer he is working in. Second, with traffic whizzing by, he's gotta have faith that the drivers are going to see his hard-hatted head. Third, the union that this man belongs to now probably prohibits smoking on the job. (UPI)

Did You Know?

Cigarette smoking in Egypt for the last fifty years has increased at the dazzling rate of 8 percent a year.

The Indian Spirit

Who knows? Maybe the Indians did have some sort of primitive cigarettes when the Pilgrims hit the shore. Let's look at it this way: The Pilgrims had been at sea for quite a while, and they didn't exactly know what they were in for. They were just sailing along toward a better life. When they saw land, they rejoiced and sent a small rowboat in before the whole group got off. These forerunners were greeted on the shore by a few Indians, who showed them around a bit.

CARVER
BRADFORD
WINSLOW
STANDISH
BREWSTER

The landing of the FATHERS *Plymouth* Dec 22 162.

After showing some of their land and visiting their little village, one of the Indians, the chief, perhaps, decided it would be a good idea to invite *all* of the Pilgrims, including the ones still sitting out on the boat, to a big feast, which they would have on the coming Thursday. The forerunning Pilgrims who had gone to shore in the little rowboat said they would go back to the ship and discuss the invitation with the others before simply accepting. They made a plan. The Pilgrims would signal the Indians from their big boat with their decision. If the sails were up they weren't coming; if they were down they would be glad to join the festivities on Thursday. They rowed back to the big ship that night in a windstorm.

You might wonder at this juncture of the story how all of this was conveyed, in the sense that these were learned people from Europe conversing with savages. But that just puts too much reality into effect, so let's proceed.

On the following Thursday at 1:00 p.m. sharp, seven rowboats were dispatched from the *Mayflower* carrying all of the inhabitants of the Pilgrim sailing ship, save the captain's galley boy, who was left to guard the ship and be sure that it remained firmly anchored. The Indians, wearing their best feathers, greeted them warmly as they came ashore. Immediately they gestured the bewildered Pilgrims to a series of large wooden tables filled with the best of their harvest: plump roasted turkeys, corn on the cob, creamed onions, giblet dressing, cranberries, and believe it or not, whipped cream created from goat's milk.

The Pilgrims were overjoyed as well as hungry. They raced toward the tables. After a short prayer administered by the ship's chaplain, the meal began and continued for hours. The newly arrived Pilgrims regaled the savages with gay stories of merry England, while the Indians shared their gnarly tales of the wilderness.

When dinner was finally over, the large integrated group

broke into smaller groups. The chief of the tribe motioned to the captain of the ship to follow him, which the captain obligingly did. They went to the chief's private tepee, not his family tepee but his officelike tepee, and they entered, with the chief taking a seat behind his birch desk and the captain reaching for and placing himself in the visitor's seat.

"Why have you brought me here, Chief?" the captain asked.

"I have a gift for you and your people. This is a gift that is based on our belief in the traditional Native American usage of tobacco in its natural state. We feel that tobacco is a powerful herb worthy of the respect it is given in Native American tradition. A natural cigarette. I hope you cherish it always." And with that, the chief handed the captain a pack of Natural American Spirits. "Go in Peace."

"I shall, Chief, and thank you for your gift."

Joe Camel

Whoever said advertising and cigarettes didn't hold hands? Joe Camel was *the* man for a while, the go-to guy when it came to cigarettes. For some reason the whole notion of spring break comes to mind.

Joe was conceived by a little-known art director in France in the 1950s. He was to spearhead a Camel blitz and began appearing on T-shirts. A few of these tees traveled back across the Atlantic, but the campaign in general fell flat and the French Camel people moved on to something new. Then a whip-smart marketing team from R.J. Reynolds rediscovered Joe in the late 1980s. Through this innocent but hip-to-the-world long-nosed camel, they began a print, billboard, and product crusade with the intention of trying to erase the image of what Camel cigarettes had become in the minds of the public—an old man's cigarette. There were lighters, beach towels, ashtrays, mugs, T-shirts, wall clocks, playing cards, ice buckets, the list goes on and on (valuable commodities on eBay). A study published in 1991 by the *Journal of the American Medical Association* stated that more five- and six-year-old children could recognize and identify Joe Camel than Mickey Mouse or Fred Flintstone. As a result of the article, the American Medical Association begged the people at R. J. Reynolds to pull the campaign; they of course refused. For years, more appeals followed, and it was not until mid-July of '97 that RJR decided to shit-can ol' Joe and move on to something new. He had a pretty good run as far as an ad man goes.

Did You Know?

Doctors led by James Sargent of the Dartmouth-Hitchcock Medical Center in Lebanon, New Hampshire, looked at the twenty-five top U.S. box-office releases for the years 1988 to 1997—250 movies in total. They found that more than 85 percent of the films featured tobacco use and that specific tobacco brands appeared in 28 percent of the movies.

The Little Man in the Red-and-Black Uniform

Johnny Roventini was exactly forty-eight inches tall, was from Brooklyn, and was a bellboy at the New Yorker Hotel in New York. One evening in April of 1933 two advertising executives were sitting in  the lobby of the New Yorker thinking about how to create a living trademark for their client, the tobacco giant Philip Morris. Above the din of lobby noise they heard the distinctive voice of Johnny Roventini every ten or fifteen minutes paging a hotel guest. It was the voice that got them, but when they finally caught up to the source and found their little bellboy, they instantly knew they had found their living trademark.

They decided to conduct one of the queerest radio auditions ever and paid Johnny one dollar to page "Mr. Philip Morris." Johnny cupped his hands to his mouth and with great enthusiasm gave a resounding "Call for Phil-lip Mor-rees." When he came back to tell the two executives that he was unable to find Mr. Morris, they in turn asked him if he would be interested in working in radio, and all he would have to do is shout "Call for Philip Morris."

Johnny said he was pretty well set at the New Yorker, was well liked and paid, and would have to think about it. "I'll have to ask my mother," he reportedly told the executives. He eventually accepted the offer but continued to work at the hotel. When showtime would approach, a Philip Morris representative would meet him at the hotel and take him to the NBC studios, then at 711 Fifth Avenue, and then return him to the New Yorker, where he continued as a page. It wasn't until December 16, 1933, that Johnny resigned from the hotel and signed a lifetime contract with Philip Morris. This is one of the few important lifetime contracts in advertising history, and remained in effect until he retired in 1974. More than a million calls for "Phil-lip Mor-rees" would be made in the years following his discovery, but the first that April evening in 1933 at the New Yorker Hotel established a vocal technique that would usher Johnny into instant folklore, and he would become as familiar to Americans as any prominent figure across the land.

During World War II, he tried to enlist in the Coast Guard Auxiliary, but his size made it impossible. He was classified as 1/2A, the only person to ever receive such a classification.

The demand for Johnny to attend such events as conventions, trade fairs, festivals, and parades became so great that four assistants, known as "Juniors," were employed to fill the demand. Johnny made the segue into television after the end of World War II, when television began replacing radio as the nation's entertainment. In the 1950s, he began appearing on such shows as *Candid Camera* with Allen Funt and *I Love Lucy* starring Lucille Ball and Desi Arnaz, and became a guest on fifteen of the top twenty shows. He was now being courted by such luminaries as Dwight and Mamie Eisenhower, who he sat with at a banquet table; Jack Dempsey; Toots Shor, who welcomed him to his inner circle at his famous eatery; Mitch Miller, who led him in song; and Jackie Gleason and his coterie of women, who walked the streets of Manhattan with him.

Wherever he went, he was immaculately dressed in his bellboy uniform; he held his head high with his chest out and smiled. He was the little man in a red and black uniform.

Drag

The most in-your-face record released in the past decade with the theme of cigarettes and smoking was from the singing Canadian cowgirl, k.d. lang. The album title was *Drag* and featured Ms. lang on the cover in an Oscar Wilde dandy suit, smoking a cigarette, of course. *Drag*, you get it? k.d. in a man's suit, and that's what you do to a cigarette. Want to make sure I didn't lose you.

k.d. lang performing at Gotham Hall in New York City in 2003, in her "I'm known for wearing this suit" men's suit. (Photograph by Mark Mainz/Getty Images)

The schema of songs on the album include: "Don't Smoke in Bed" (right! A lament from an under-sexed wife no doubt leaving her husband with a loving warning), the Hollies' "The Air That I Breathe" (Canadian north winds), "Smoke Rings" (where a sad smoker is blowing smoke rings that bring on smoke dreams of the lover that has run off to become an Eve Arden salesperson outside of Albuquerque), "My Last Cigarette" (in which she is singing to her professed lover that she is indeed her last—her last cigarette), and then the kicker . . . the "Theme from Valley of the Dolls." Her singing on this album sounds like the droning of an opium queen pulling herself out of a wet sleeping bag in a Seattle basement in the early '90s, but the instrumentation gets as close as any music ever will to resembling the curlicues of smoke rising from an ashtray.

Did You Know?

Anger management: Irritated with traffic gridlock? Well, if you lived in Northern California during the late 1980s you could show your displeasure by smoking a Gridlock cigarette. Introduced to San Francisco Bay Area motorists in 1988, Gridlock, "the Commuter's Cigarette," was made by Philip Morris as a private label for a chain of convenience stores.

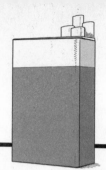

Camel Profile

The Camel smoker, a filter, a light man, or even a wide guy is your basic take-no-prisoners traditionalist. He waters his backyard by hand, avoiding sprinkler systems, drinks his American beer from the bottle, and even though he goes to bed late he is an early riser. He is competitive and watches the ESPN scores at the bottom of his television screen, enjoys participating in nonball and target sports, and wears khakis in the summer months and bright down vests in the winter. He boasts of his sit-up stamina, rarely dates the same woman more than three times, and listens to vintage metal in his weekend pickup as he just "drives around."

MALE NAMES
Fred, Bob, Craig, Monty, Chuck (mustache optional), Dick, Zeke

FEMALE NAMES
None

OCCUPATIONS
Credit manager for Best Buy, minor league baseball player, electric utility load dispatcher, artistic welder, Boise Cascade paper salesman

AGE RANGE
18–49

AWARDS AND PRIZES

NRA Sharpshooter safety award, Voit scuba gear finalist for offshore duration testing, Gillette promo gift package from local Wells Fargo bank, work attendance record, Staples "Pick to Win" contestant and semifinalist

RELIGION

Christian

EDUCATION

Couple of years of state college, then hitchhiked around America to check things out

SALARY RANGE

$55,000

LAST BOOK READ

Freakonomics by Stephen D. Levitt and Stephen J. Dubner

Devoted Camel smoker and author Marc Spitz smoking in front of one of his favorite watering holes in Manhattan. Spitz says, "I enjoying smoking in front of bars . . . you meet the coolest people there, and . . . they all smoke and pretty much like the same music."

> **"Coffee and smoking are the last great addictions."**
>
> —LARA FLYNN BOYLE

Looking for Love

It's ten o'clock on a Sunday night. The weekend is over, you've given up on the Sunday night movie, you're tired and think you should probably go to bed, but you think why not one more, and guess what . . . you're out of cigarettes!

Everybody's been through this type of situation. You can't believe you would be so absentminded, but then you can't believe with a habit like yours, coupled with your forgetfulness, that there isn't at least one cigarette somewhere in the house. There's gotta be.

The first thing to do is to try to borrow or bum one from someone else. But that's usually not possible. Fellow family members usually don't like to be awoken, and neighbors, unless that one kitchen light is still on, are not going to greet you with open arms . . . "Sure, come on in. What flavor would you like?"

So the search begins. Think. Where do you usually keep them? Everyone has an area: on top of the dresser with your keys, in the kitchen on the counter where you have your coffee in the morning, in the front hall, or that special drawer in the living room where you keep cigarettes for the guests.

Struck out?

Next step. What were you wearing the last time you remember having cigarettes? A coat, aha! Check the coat in the front closet. Not there. Check the other coats while you're there, top inside pockets as well as breast and side pockets. How about your other coats in the bedroom? Check all the pockets, thoroughly. You might find a loose one that fell out of a pack. Top pocket of your shirt? Still nothing? Walking down the street to the store or getting in the car seems a bit much at this hour.

It's twelve fifteen, and now you would really like a cigarette. You are now Dracula looking for blood with the dawn breaking. You'd like a cigarette while you look for your cigarettes. Now the final grand search, the mine sweep, sonar probing along the ocean floor, begins before you have to submit to the inevitable.

> **"For the first time in history, sex is more dangerous than the cigarette afterward."**
>
> —Jay Leno

Check the obvious places again briefly. Check around the areas where you usually smoke. One might have dropped out of the pack accidentally. Look under the beds, sofas, armchairs, and tables. No luck. Check the empty packs in the garbage can to see if you left one in by mistake.

Sit down, breathe deeply, and think before succumbing to the inevitable. Give yourself a full minute or two.

It's now one ten. You haven't found a cigarette, so ... start checking the ashtrays and god help you, the garbage pail, for the largest and most pristine butts. It's crude and rude, but it's a cigarette and you promise yourself you'll never, and emphasize *never*, make this mistake again.

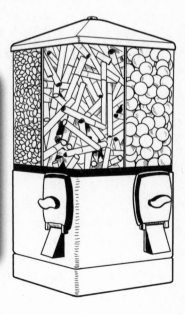

My Cigarette

My cigarette! The amulet
    That charms afar unrest and sorrow,
The magic want that, far beyond
    To-day, can conjure up to-morrow.
Like love's desire, thy crown of fire
    So softly with the twilight blending;
And ah! Meseems a poet's dreams
    Are in thy wreaths of smoke ascending.

My cigarette! Can I forget?
    How Kate and I, in sunny weather,
Sat in the shade the elm-tree made
    And rolled the fragrant weed together?
I at her side, beatified,
    To hold and guide her fingers willing;
She's rolling slow the paper's snow
    Putting my heart in with the filling.

My cigarette! I see her yet,
    The white smoke from her red lips curling
Her dreaming eyes, her soft replies,
    Her gentle sighs, her laughter purling;
Ah, dainty roll, whose parting soul
    Ebbs out in many a snowy billow;
I, too, would burn, if I could earn
    Upon her lips, so soft a pillow.

Ah, cigarette! The gay coquette
    Had long forgot the flame she lighted . . .

—CHARLES FLETCHER LUMMIS

This poem was written by Charles Fletcher Lummis and published in 1879. Lummis was a precocious poet who walked from Ohio to California in 1884 in a pair of knickerbockers and plain old street shoes. He gained recognition from the American public with his letters about his adventures along the way. Upon arriving in Los Angeles, he landed a job at the *Los Angeles Times*. Born a New Englander, he gained a deep appreciation for both the natural beauty and cultural diversity of the Southwest, where he remained until he died. His best poem is "My Cigarette," and it rightfully brings forth two of his obsessions: tobacco and women.

Did You Know?

In 1930, Larus & Brothers, a manufacturer of pipe tobaccos—namely a brand called Edgeworth—launched a new cigarette that was composed of the same harsh pipe tobacco mixture. It became Joseph Stalin's favorite cigarette and then became the rage among the trendy intellectuals of the time.

Other Uses

Besides the obvious uses of cigarettes—namely, smoking them—there are a variety of other uses for them as well. First of all, regard them as a small fire source; they yield smoke and can be easily concealed. Second, they are little cylindrical objects that in various combinations can act as something else. Consider the following list, then come up with some of your own.

1. During the Fourth of July holiday period, New Year's Eve, or any other celebratory event, use a lighted cigarette to ignite your various fireworks displays.

2. Entertain the elderly and/or children in the dark with the glowing embers of your cigarette. Use several in each hand and rotate arms quickly.

3. 100 millimeter or longer cigarettes can act as excellent substitutes for either building pieces like Lincoln Logs or for games of pickup sticks. It is advised not to use burning cigrettes in this case.

4. Tease your pets by trying to have them inhale a cigarette as you do. Blow smoke directly at them and watch them scamper. Attach burning cigarettes to cages and watch your pet cower in the opposite corner.

5. Fool your teachers at the university by exchanging the chalk on the lip of the black board with cigarettes. Use nonfilter for best results.

6. Because of the slow-burning nature of cigarettes they can be utilized in a number of ways as ignition fuses for small to large incendiary devices.

7. At your next big poker game, instead of conventional red, white, and blue chips, use a variety of cigarettes. Since poker is usually played in smoke-filled environments anyway, why not make it easy to enjoy your rewards immediately upon winning.

8. Blowing smoke rings (see page 124) is an art that takes hours of practice and many many packs of cigarettes to perfect. Beautifully exhaled smoke rings are very effective in many situations, such as on a first date, at children's parties, or just sitting by one's self.

In the late 1930s tobacco advertisers started turning to the comic book form of drawn paneled ads. This was combined with the wisdom of someone famous, in this instance Chick Meehan, a three-sport athlete at Christian Brothers Academy in Syracuse. "Chick," I'll have you know, was inducted into the Greater Syracuse Sports Hall of Fame. Chick no doubt inhaled a couple of truckloads of Camels in his lifetime, and he also used them to pick up chicks at football games by convincing them they would give them energy. Energy for what, Chick?

"Smoking is one of the leading causes of statistics."

—FLETCHER KNEBEL

"I'm not perfect, I do drink. I do smoke. Carson [Carson Daly] can't go out and get messed up, he can't smoke in front of kids——he's the face of MTV, and he has to be good. But me? I can.**"**

—Tara Reid

Did You Know?

Smoking is prohibited on streets in some areas of Tokyo; hence smokers retreat into smoking lounges.

Party Treat

Here's a little party treat that'll delight the younger folks in the crowd and bring back pleasant memories for the senior citizens.

Before arriving at a party, secure a straight pin (it can be a sewing pin as well) about two inches in length. Stick it directly into the cigarette from the tobacco end. Push it all the way in. Use a filter cigarette; a nonfilter can get pretty dicey. Stick it in your pack and save it for the appropriate moment.

When executing the trick, light your cigarette and keep it in your mouth. Act nonchalant and don't speak. To the amazement of the crowd, the ash will grow longer and longer, but it will never fall off.

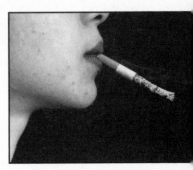

Hold the cigarette between you and don't move. The ash grows

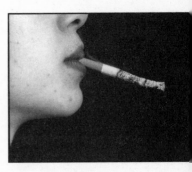

grows . . .

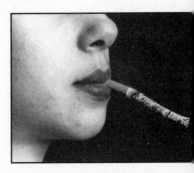

. . . and grows!

Pets

Teaching your pets how to smoke cigarettes or to become familiar with some of the various tricks and rituals involved in the cigarette smoking process takes time, patience, and a lot of stamina. In general, animals shy away from cigarettes unless they are trained from a very early age to think that cigarettes can be fun. Once they learn this, it's fun to smoke along with them or use them to abet your habit.

A trained rabbit in Russia that was being used in medical research actually developed a habit after five years and was accustomed to smoking six or seven cigarettes a day. (UPI)

The animal psychologist that is holding the cigarette for the fish trained over twenty-three different species, many in his home laboratory, to smoke. Wonder what he did with his information?

Frederick the Great was the frog's name, and at the time he was the only known frog in captivity to smoke. He was trained to smoke by Martin Walter, a veteran Indian fighter. (Acme)

A few things come to mind here. Did the parakeet light the match? Will the man light his cigarette? Will the man offer the parakeet a cigarette and light his? (UPI)

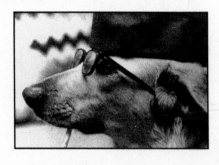

This is King, and his master taught him how to smoke. He is wearing a getup that he will wear to his master's late husband's Memorial Day service. A New York cigarette company offered his master $15,000 for King, but she refused. She said she might let him do some advertising, but . . . the price would have to be right.

Ai Ai, a twenty-six-year-old chimpanzee, enjoying a cigarette after a meal in her glass enclosure at the zoo in Xi'an, in central China's Shaanxi province, in August 2005. The zookeepers claimed she took up the habit after her mate died. China is home to one in three of the world's human smokers and is the world's largest producer of tobacco. The World Health Organization (WHO) estimates there are 350 million smokers in China, or some 36 percent of its population. (AFP/Getty Images)

Lighting Cigarettes

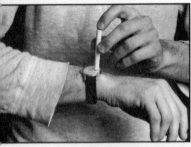

So round, so firm, so fully packed, the adage used to go. A lot of guys like to be sure, though. Sure of what, I'm not quite sure. You will see a lot of people tapping their packs of cigarettes right after they have bought them. They always have that "I'm driving this bus and no one is gonna get killed" face. They are confident and self-assured. These pictures illustrate the single cigarette packing method. Hold the cigarette lightly and don't force it too much or you'll break it. Repeat the action several times. It suggests perfection. Now you are ready to fire that bugger up.

Lighting a cigarette is probably the most important step in the whole smoking process. If you don't light the cigarette, what is the point? It won't work, it won't smoke. And you want it to smoke because that's where the pleasure is.

Since the beginning of time, when the first of us humans reared up off our hind legs and decided to get civilized, fire has been something we have utilized for keeping warm, cooking food, destroying things, illuminating, and so forth. Cavemen, as lore has it, struck rocks together, then the Indian person, a slightly more civilized biped, learned to rub sticks together to create fire, and then sulfur came along and abetted the process by enabling man to invent matches, and that takes us all the way to today, where there are so many ways to light things it just seems like it always was that way.

Now back to the matter at hand, lighting cigarettes. Everyone has their favorite technique, their favorite lighter, matches, or embers, and a good cigarette smoker always knows how to get one lit. The following modern, contemporary examples are just to refresh your memory, to keep the flame lit, as it were.

The common matchbox.   From another cigarette.
Makes you feel like a cowboy. Great conversation starter.

The colonial method, from a candle. Suggests a certain continuity with the enviroment.

From a burning ember. Camper's delight! Or a method employed by "Don't worry, Mom. I'm in the den talking with Dad about graduate school" twenty-year-old.

The disposable lighter, probably the most common method used in the world today.

Matchbook. When more people smoked, more shops and restaurants had a box of matchbooks by the counter, often under a small sign that read "For Our 'Matchless' Friends."

Got a stick match but no place to light it? Use your . . . imagination.

Zippo, king of lighters. Favorite of the G.I.'s in both World Wars, Korea, and Vietnam.

Off the stove, the morning-after method.

The car lighter. A rare find these days.

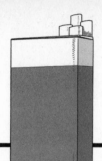

Marlboro Profile

For people who smoke Marlboros, nothing is harder than being without them. These smokers smoke while riding horses, in the bathrooms of movie houses, in their cars pulling out from Wendy's—in short, everywhere they can. Marlboro smokers are a rough bunch, preferring taverns to cocktail lounges. Country music is their Muzak; they butter their bread with real butter and keep extra packs of cigarettes in their glove compartments. Their language is peppered with four-letter words; a tight T-shirt doesn't bother them; they have no fear of kicking a malfunctioning jukebox, and have no intention of ever going to Europe. Marlboros are for *real* people.

MALE NAMES
Bill, Emmett, Hank, Mack, Roy, Vic, Chuck

FEMALE NAMES
Nan, Trix (or Trixie), Tina, Liz, Juanita, Pat, Sherry, Tammy

OCCUPATIONS
Construction worker, forever teenager, fish-and-tackle store employee, coal miner, secretary at tire distributor, Shriners,

Come to where the flavor is. Come to Marlboro Country.

short-order cook at Popeye's, housewife with many children and no help, movie stunt extra

AGE RANGE
11–35

AWARDS AND PRIZES
none

RELIGION
Little Baptist stuff way back when

EDUCATION
Tenth or eleventh grade; weapons management certificate, U.S. Army; first place at Subway employees' apple bobbing contest at company picnic

SALARY RANGE
$12,500–$22,500

LAST BOOK READ
Hell's Angel by Sonny Barger

Smoking in the old West was a pretty common thing. Cowboy slang for a book of cigarette papers was "the bible," which was used to roll Bull Durham tobacco.

Posing

An essential part of the whole cigarette smoking ritual is holding the burning unit. All smokers develop their own method, their own pose. It is how they want to present themselves to the world, their posture, their masquerade. Cigarette grips are like fingerprints, they're all different in nature and effect. People talk, people gesticulate, people dismiss, admit, honor, and acknowledge the world with the way they hold and use their cigarettes.

The Conventioneer

These smokers never vary. Their cigarettes are firmly gripped between the index and second fingers. They shut their eyes slightly or squint when they take a drag, seemingly floating off to another world. The message related is: *I smoke cigarettes. I don't break the rules. My IRA is in good shape. I'm conventional.*

The Effete

This smoking crowd really uses their cigarettes for special effects; like a run-on sentence, their cigarettes serve as punctuation. The eyes of the room are usually riveted on the effete smoker's batonlike mastery of the cigarette. They are light smokers, preferring to smoke only after seated and served at dinner parties or during cocktail parties honoring the music of Nat King Cole. The message related is: *My dear, of course Alfred will relinquish what is not his.*

Humphrey Bogart

Tough, unassuming smokers, they constantly dare their audience to answer back in any way, shape, or form. It is as if they are constantly waiting for a train to Chicago on a rainy platform. This type of smoker is also quite proud of the stains on his hands and fingers. They are reminders of his insensitive and coarse manner. His cigarette serves as a kind of cop's nightstick. The message related is: *That's right, Bud, I said tomorrow!*

The Cleopatra Look

They're usually she-types who fiddle with their cigarettes. Because of their fidgety and flighty manner, they can't decide upon an actual, practical grip. They use both hands, probably don't inhale, smoke different brands of ultra lights constantly, and they are guilty of borrowing a lot of cigarettes from others as well. The message related is: *Right in the middle of everything, my gosh, the lights went out and I was forced to look for candles again for the second time this summer.*

James Dean

They have a cigarette in their hand because it is simply their nature. They have to. Otherwise, the image, the tough guy with no life insurance and a barking mutt in the back of his pickup, wouldn't be complete. They drag deeply when they inhale, but their burning cigarette hangs like a broken tree limb in their hand. The message related is: *I really don't give a damn if Carol is moving back to California or not.*

The Novelist

They usually smoke at night and outside, and, most important, by themselves. Their cigarette is their best friend but they still want to conceal it. They are constantly reflecting, and they wipe their mouth with the palm of their hand a lot. They flick their burning cigarette a lot, but when they smoke they are never talking to anyone but themselves. The message related is (ruminating): *If I left my BMV up here for a couple more months I could. . .*

These are all ways *not* to hold a cigarette.

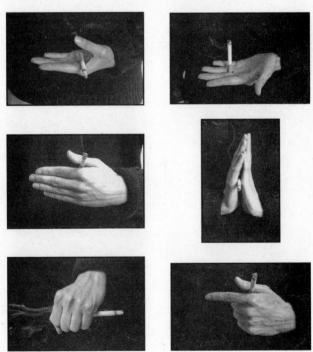

Raymond Loewy

Lucky Raymond

There lived a young man named Loewy
Whose art and design was quite showy
From the Pennsylvania Railroad to the Studebaker car
His logos and designs were seen near and far.

New bottles and cans Coca-Cola received
Logos and trademarks all well conceived
For Lucky Strike's cigarette design he decided
That the image would work on either sided.

— JAMES FITZGERALD

The Lucky Strike logo was designed and created by the infamous American industrial designer Raymond Loewy. When the president of the American Tobacco Company and the manufacturer of Lucky Strike, George Washington Hill, heard that Loewy didn't approve of the cigarette pack graphics, a $50,000 bet was made that Loewy could not do any better. Loewy won the wager when George Hill liked the new streamlined version of the Lucky Strike package that Loewy created.

Rolling Your Own

Creating your own cigarettes by rolling them is a simple process once you get it down. Practice makes perfect; a little practice and you'll be able to do it in no time with your eyes shut. Plus, if it fits into your new look, you'll be considered cool and frugal all at once. You'll be Bob Dylan on the cover of *The Times They Are A-Changin'*, you'll be regarded as a self-sufficient DIY'er with attitude who smokes, a pioneer of the twenty-first century, Emma Goldman with tobacco, and . . . you'll be saving a ton of money.

There are two methods of rolling your own cigarettes. The illustrations feature a little rolling machine. The other method is bareback, with just your hands. Use the little machine to roll a couple dozen at home. People ask too many questions when you pull the machine out in public, things like, "Where did you get that?" or "How much did that gizmo cost ya?" Your machine-rolled smokes can also be housed in creative packages; make your own or use classy cigarette cases.

In rolling your own with just your hands, be aware that this process is fascinating to everybody around you. You'll be bombarded with questions here as well. Just do your thing, establish your style, and act like you are above everyone else.

Machine-Rolling Method

Step 1

Step 2

Step 3

Step 4

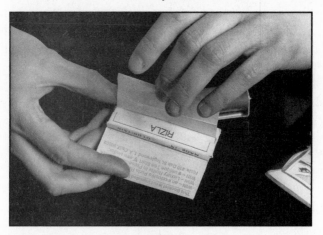

Step 5

Step 6

Step 7

Step 8

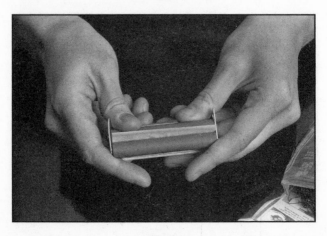

Step 9

Step 10

Step 11

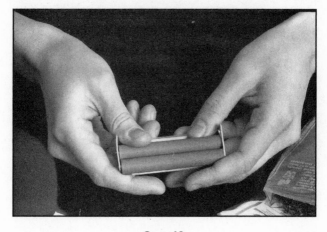

Step 12

Step 13

Step 14

The happy smoker with her freshly rolled cigarette

Sean Penn

Sean Penn, star of stage and screen, was certainly not one of the king's men in Toronto in September of 2006. He lit a cigarette at a Toronto International Film Festival press conference while promoting his latest film, as he had done at previous festivals. But alas, the laws had changed. Smoking is now banned in all public places in the state of Ontario, including outdoor arenas and company cars. After the infringement, in which Penn faced a steep $600 fine, Toronto's medical officer of health planned not only to write to Penn outlining the requirements in Ontario but also planned to write to the Toronto International Film Festival organizers

urging them to ensure that all future visiting Hollywood types follow the letter of the law. The medical officer also wrote in his letter to Penn that the actor was more than welcome to come back next year and that he hoped by then Penn would have "kicked the habit."

Sean Penn, during the *All the King's Men* press conference at the Toronto International Film Festival held at the Sutton Place Hotel in September 2006 in Toronto. (Evan Agostini/Getty Images)

A Day Without

Throughout the duration of World War II, Chesterfield advertisements regularly featured glamour photographs of a Chesterfield Girl of the Month, usually a fashion model or a Hollywood star, such as Rita Hayworth, Rosalind Russell, or Betty Grable. The model above was featured in February in the early 1940s.

Every smoker thinks about how one day, one day in the far future, the bell will ring and he will just stop smoking cigarettes. Easy to say, very easy to say. And once in a while, it may be the result of a new significant other, an illness, a religious obligation, or some such baggage. You are forced to go for an extended time, like twenty-four hours (eight to ten of which you will be sleeping) without a cigarette. And those days . . . in a fishbowl with your mind racing along, yo-yoing back and forth with a single thought . . . just one cigarette, just one blasted drag.

On one occasion, I decided to go a day without smoking and really let my body go and my mind follow. I picked a date, about two weeks ahead, and did it.

My day started with the immediate thought *Oh, yeah, I promised myself a week or two ago and again last night not to smoke today.* That dissipated pretty quickly, and I purposefully did not go into the kitchen right away because . . . well, the coffeepot was there and you know what goes with coffee. So, I got into some exercises, and I started doing these kinda lame jumping jacks and they turned into touching my toes almost, and by that time the blood was flowing and it was time for some sit-ups. Boy, it was coming on now . . . I was just feeling so healthy. I ran quickly to the shower, and that's a nonsmoking area so the brain trigger was not blinking, and in fact the idea of smoking just went away for a while. Four minutes later, getting dressed, breathing deeply, I thought I'd just get out the door and go and it would be all right. I'd leave the lighters behind, maybe walk a new way, take my time . . . jeeze, it was only 7:45 and I was already out the door.

I did go a new way to work, had some juice and a muffin of sorts along the way. I was being leisurely and not thinking about you know what, but the truth was I was thinking that maybe just one now and then quit for the rest of the day, but that seemed ridiculous. I would have to buy a pack, and then what, throw the others away? No, maybe I could bum one. My mind was racing with these thoughts and then suddenly I got to work. Okay, nice mental distraction, and since I couldn't smoke in the building anyway, I'd be okay until noon. Noon! Oh, I hoped I didn't schedule a lunch with a smoker! I checked and saw the slot blank, good, but maybe not so good because I would be alone and . . . I decided to call someone who does not smoke and schedule lunch. It worked; we were meeting, and that would kill another hour in this day that now seemed to be stretching out into a month.

Lunch was fine, at a smoke-free environment with a smoke-free friend. I had a dessert and skipped the coffee, stretching the oasis time out a bit. I walked briskly back to work with my mind racing on all the things I could fill the afternoon up with. I actually got a little semi-high in my new oxygenated state, I was feeling the energy. . . .

The afternoon passed and I dreaded the evening now, the smoking lamp would not be lit, and I started considering the options: a movie . . . no smoking there; another eating establishment, safe grounds; home for a series of showers, but all those triggers around the house, the smoking chair, the window, no? Home was not a good idea. I decided to take a long walk and see what happened.

When you are not smoking and especially if you have just quit, you notice all the people who are smoking and their curious little habits and how some look downright weird holding a burning something in their hand or pinched between their lips. And then you start wondering what you look like when you smoke, and wondering if people look at you. Another passing thought as the sun is going down.

> **"I wouldn't mind seeing opera die. Ever since I was a boy, I regarded opera as a ponderous anachronism, almost the equivalent of smoking."**
>
> —FRANK LLOYD WRIGHT

I walked what seemed like forever and settled in at a restaurant I'd never been to before with a few magazines, a crossword puzzle. You get the drift. I was going to stretch this one out. Had one drink, sipped it and read away, finally ordered and ate slowly, more dessert, coffee, which I decided after I had ordered it may not be the best idea, numero uno taste trigger, but I tricked myself and had a decaf and it was okay.

I left the joint and saw that it was edging up on eight o'clock. Almost eight! So much time on my hands. A full evening lay in front of me. All this time and no cigarettes! The logic now led me to: You have not had one all day, it's been a good day, you deserve one, just one. Think of all those cigarettes you had before today, how is one going to hurt you? Who was this talking to me? The bad side of town was rearing its head.

When I got home, I decided television would do the trick for a while. It marched the time by, and that seemed to be what this was all about. The cigarettes used to measure my time. I'd have this one then go in and pay the bills, or one more cigarette then go to bed. . . . Television did it; I of course was switching channels as fast as a teenager, but not to worry, my confident side was starting to kick in. It was after ten, sleep soon and I would have completed the day. A day without cigarettes.

In bed, sleep didn't exactly come on quickly. It was no Lunesta ad, in other words. Many different positions, arranging the pillows. *You know*, I thought, *maybe this will work, no pajamas tonight, nature boy, a non-smoking healthy boy with lots of energy.* And that worked for a bit, but then it was back out to the kitchen for a couple of big tall glasses of water, a little pacing, and then back to bed.

The end of the story is that I did eventually fall off into the lightest sleep since Amelia Earhart dozed off in her cockpit, but I made it through the day and will someday do it again. Someday in the near, near future. Right.

Did You Know?

A recently discovered tobacco industry document illustrates the role Hollywood plays in tobacco marketing and promotion. Marlboro cigarettes accounted for 40 percent of the brands depicted in films since 1998.

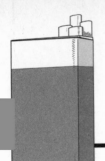

Carlton Profile

Carltons are smoked by people who made good grades in high school, part their hair, and feel a little guilty that they smoke at all. They group together at parties, smoke and rid their common guilt by constantly reading the impressive statistics on their cigarette packs. During the fall months they turn on football games but don't watch them, preferring instead the solace of reading a bestselling hardcover book instead. They dutifully attend their swanky college reunions, eat good breakfasts full of fiber and fruit, and tote their kids up in the BMW to see Grandma and Grandpa at the lake every summer.

MALE NAMES
Archibald ("Arch" to the guys at the squash club), Charles, Gerard, James, Pierce, Raney, Cyril

FEMALE NAMES
Colleen, Jacqueline, Meredith, Penelope, Victoria, Phoebe

OCCUPATIONS
Orthodontist, aerospace engineer, stock market analyst (including hedge funds), junior league leader, wine magazine columnist, management training specialist, and compensation analyst

AGE RANGE
32–45

AWARDS AND PRIZES
American Airlines 150,000 mile club, *Kenyon Review* poetry award, various piscatorial achievements in the United States and Europe, Pottery Barn citation for creative needlework design patterns, UNICEF chapter chairman

RELIGION
Presbyterian, Erastian

EDUCATION
BA and BS across the board, with some postgraduate studies and MBA or MAs in specific job-related fields

SALARY RANGE
$250,000-plus

LAST BOOK READ
YOU: The Owner's Manual: An Insider's Guide to the Body That Will Make You Healthier and Younger by Mehmet C. Oz and Michael F. Roizen

Did You Know?

Nicotine is named for a sixteenth-century Frenchman, Jean Nicot, who took tobacco leaves imported from America to Catherine de Medici as a cure for her migraines.

Slogans

A slogan is an attention-getting word or phrase used to publicize something, as a campaign or product, and no one was better at it than the Madison Avenue ad men who created campaigns for cigarettes. They were featured everywhere, in print ads, on the radio, on television, with giveaway buttons, on billboards, you name it. And many of them were trademarked. Here are but just a few.

forever and ever

"It's toas

Come to where the flavor is	Marlboro
Just what the doctor ordered	L&M
Not a cough in a carload	Old Gold
I'd rather fight than switch	Tareyton
Enjoy a cooler kind of mild	Kool Milds
Blow some my way	Chesterfield
It's what's up front that counts	Winston
It's toasted	Lucky Strike
100% additive-free tobacco	Natural American Spirit
Taste me! Taste me! Come on and taste me!	Doral
Tastes good like a cigarette should	Winston
They do satisfy	Chesterfield
Wherever particular people congregate	Pall Mall
Try the taste that's springtime fresh	Salem
The fellow that introduced me to Camels was certainly some friend of mine	Camel

We've got the taste that's right, right	
any time of the day	Viceroy
You can't take the country out of Salem	Salem
I'd walk a mile for a Camel	Camel
You've come a long way, baby	Virginia Slims
Be happy, go lucky	Lucky Strike
Strike up the mild	Montclair
This is the one they'll have to beat	Carlton
Farewell to the ugly cigarette	Eve
For digestion's sake	Camel

Did You Know?

A 1928 Lucky Strike ad featured Amelia Earhart, who supposedly carried Luckies aboard the airplane *Friendship* when she crossed the Atlantic Ocean.

Professional photographer and devoted cigarette smoker Louis DeCarlo enjoying one of his hand-rolled Golden Virginia roll-ups with silver Rizla skins.

Smoke Rings

Frontal views. Notice lip position and the amount of smoke pouring forth.

Some people can blow them, some people can't or don't want to. Some people want to be able to blow them, so they practice and practice. After a while, hours and hours and packs and packs later, they can blow smoke rings, even if it's only in their own particular way.

To blow smoke rings from your mouth, the key is to push the smoke out with your tongue with an ever so small push from your lungs. The art requires incredible tongue control. And not too much lung effort.

Smoke rings require a lot of smoke. Like, duh, but what you do is, you puff on your cigarette for a while, building a reservoir, a small little Lake Erie of smoke in your mouth. Don't inhale. Cigarettes are the hardest smoking apparatus for creating rings; cigars are much better. Thicker smoke.

The speed at which you exhale controls the size. The slower, the bigger the ring. Big, thick Seventy-sixth Infantry howitzer cannon rings. Faster respiration creates small little begrimed halos like Magritte skies. Whatever effect you are trying to create is established by the exhaling.

No two smoke-ringers are the same. Some ringers can blow only one heavy unit that seems to hang in the air for a long time. Some blow a series of little rings that seem to follow after each other until they dissipate. And yet others, who have really perfected the art, can form little chains by just bending their necks.

Smoke rings are great for children's parties, board meetings where you have lost interest in the goings-on, or for your own private moments, when you feel like being more creative in your smoking than simply inhaling and exhaling.

Four views of the ring process. Notice how the smoker, in an almost Houdini-like trance, concentrates on the rings themselves.

Ninety-eight-year-old Dr. Maurice J. Lewi, president of the New York College of Podiatry in 1955, shows us his method. (New York Journal/American)

Smokin' Behind Bars

Jail ain't no fun. But if you get caught at something, well you gotta pay for it. Smoking cigarettes in jail is something almost *everybody* does. Ya almost kinda have to. Cigarettes are better than money in the clink 'cause ya cain't smoke money. In fact, cigarettes is money in jail. If yer smart and use 'em right, they'll get you a few more minutes in the yard, maybe a couple of more beans on yer plate . . . or a new Kmart pillow. I knew one guy who got hisself a television set with a VCR thing in it, with just trading cigarettes. The guy he got it from died a little bit after that but that don't matter. Myself, I smoke Chesterfields. They're the longest one going that we can get our hands on. You can also break 'em in half and get two cigarettes out of them too. Most of us smoke them or Pall Malls . . . but I like the taste of the Chesterfields a lot more. And we save the butts too. The man passes out cigarettes sometimes and guys get 'em sent in from their girlfriends and stuff but your butt pile can get you through some long nights. They get to be your friends. I smoke a lotta cigarettes and if the good Lord ever sees fit to gittin' me outta this hole, I'll probably smoke cigarettes on the outside too.

—CHARLES "BUBBA" ROTWEILLER
San Quentin, California

On July 1, 2006, California adopted a new policy prohibiting cigarette smoking in all of the state's prisons. The legislation was pushed through on the premise that it was a way to save the taxpaying public millions of

> **"It's kind of gratifying to see that *my* cigarette is America's choice, too."**
> —JOHN WAYNE

dollars in health care costs and, this is the part that is interesting, to improve the health of prisoners. Now, try explaining this new law to someone who has probably smoked his or her entire life and is now in prison serving an extended life sentence. The tobacco ban on at Folsom State Prison has sent tobacco prices through the tin roof. Cigarettes or loose tobacco that went for $11 in May of '06 was going for $200 three months later. Prisons with tobacco bans now have a new network of tobacco brokers, middlemen, and enforcers assigned to collect debts from smokers. One prisoner was quoted as saying that tobacco was going to cost more than illegal drugs. California is not the first state to pass this type of law. Maine banned smoking in prisons in 2000. The result: assaults quadrupled.

Did You Know?

Between 1941 and 1945, the war years, 250 billion cigarettes were sent overseas. President Franklin Roosevelt reclassed tobacco as an "essential" crop and draft boards were directed to defer farmers to ensure maximum output.

Smokin' in Front of Bars

Way back in 1590, Pope Urban VII, during his short papal reign, introduced the world's first known public smoking ban. He threatened to excommunicate anyone from the Catholic Church who used tobacco in the vestibule of or inside a church, whether it be by chewing it, smoking it with a pipe, or sniffing it in powdered form through their noses. Cigarettes were not a commodity then.

The Trail's End Saloon in Barnsdall, Oklahoma. You can bet they ain't gonna run some whiskey-drinkin' cowpoke outta this joint for smoking a Marlboro or three.

Then it seems everybody was cool with both tobacco and smoking until the end of the twentieth century, when medical research studies on the health risks of tobacco smoking started leaking out to the press and the general public. Surgeon generals began appearing on television, the advertising seemed to be disappearing, rock stars were no longer being pictured with cigarettes. The tobacco industry panicked. They immediately launched a series of courtesy awareness campaigns. "Mind if I smoke here around you?"

I could get into a whole day-by-day history of banning smoking, in public spaces, and then finally in bars, but it is boring. Let's just say it spread across the world like a prairie fire, politicians jumped on the ban-wagon, environmentalists rallied, mothers, the medical community, everyone who did not smoke took careful aim at the smokers.

For those smokers today who live in cities, this new banishment has reduced us down to the status of lepers. The upstanding nonsmokers have us standing in front of establishments to smoke and complain with other smokers, surrounded by those weird long-necked ashtrays with quippy phrases on them like "Place Your Butts Here!"

Through wind, snow, rain, and blistering heat, there we stand. Those who live outside cities and depend on cars for all their transportation now use their cars as their new smoking lounges. Won't be long before they ban smoking cigarettes in cars.

Outdoor sign for the infamous Smoking Club in Yucatan, Mexico.

My solution. How about smoking bars, bars just for cigarette smokers, and let's get the tobacco industry involved. Set these new bars up with designated areas like the supermarkets do with vegetables and cheeses and soda. But in these new Cigaretterias, cigarettes would be sold one by one, in clusters, in packs, or in cartons and served just like drinks. There could be, for example, a cowboy saloon area where Marlboro Reds would be served along with the shots of bourbon and domestic beers. Then there could be a breezy Marc Jacobs area with Pottery Barn settees and pillows adjacent to it for the Marlboro Light crowd. Each cigarette would have its area and you could bounce around sampling or go to your brand's spot and stick it out with your fellow smokers. An Arabian setting complete with asps coming out of earthenware vases in a pasha's tent for the Camel crowd, a European train station for the Gauloises smokers, a dental office for Kent smokers, a swimming pool setting with club sandwiches and ice tea for the Salem folks . . . the list goes on. And all of it, this multi-environed smoking Mecca, would be underwritten and paid for by the Big Tobacco companies. No one would offend anyone else; it'd be one big happy smoking crowd. The one rule would be that if you didn't smoke, you'd have to go out and stand in front of the place.

Did You Know?

Not only did Philip Morris arrange for Lois Lane (Margot Kidder) to smoke Marlboros in *Superman II*, but the film also included a classic fight scene in which Superman and the bad guys throw a Marlboro truck back and forth across Lexington Avenue. This truck was produced solely for the movie and is in use nowhere else.

Smoking in Arabia

Sunni Muslims sit outside the Abdul Kader al-Gilani mosque enjoying a cigarette before being called in for Friday noon prayer in central Baghdad, January 2006. (KARIM SAHIB/AFP/Getty Images)

The majority of Arab adults smoke. Both men and women consider smoking an integral part of adult behavior, although women are rarely seen smoking in public. If one wishes to smoke in the presence of Arabs, it is important to be prepared to offer a cigarette to everyone in the group. It is considered impolite not to offer. Conversely, it is not considered appropriate to ask an Arab not to smoke.

Smoking cigarettes often interferes with an Arab's life and worship. Smoking is clearly forbidden during the daytime fast of Ramadan. Many addicted Arabian smokers spend their fasting days sleeping, cranky and short-tempered, just counting the hours until they can have their cigarette fix at sunset. The heaviest smokers will wait outside the mosque door for the *adhan*, and break their fast by lighting up before taking even food or water.

Allah says, "... *But spend not wastefully (your wealth) in the manner of a spendthrift. Verily spendthrifts are brothers of the devils* ..." (Surah al-Israa' 17:26–27). And in an authentic hadith, the tradition based on reports of the sayings and activities of Muhammad, the Prophet (peace be upon him) said: "*Allah hates for you three things: gossiping, begging, and wasting money.*"

He—Allah, that is—didn't mention cigarettes, which is probably what gives the Arabs license to smoke like runaway locomotives.

Did You Know?

A tablespoon of tobacco seeds sows six acres of land.

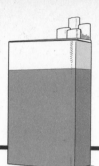

Salem Profile

Although they have been put forth as "fresh as the out-of-doors," Salems are usually smoked on the run or in crowded situations (where smoking is allowed) by very serious smokers. Menthol smokers. Salem-ites are slick, they've got it all figured out when you see them from afar in their polyester coats and heavily made-up faces. They wear slip-on shoes for convenience, shop on the Internet for bargains, but prefer to grace the aisles of large, multi-aisled, well-lighted superstores. Their vacations are strictly Fodor-driven four-night, five-day visits to safe, by the beach, places. No pets allowed. They buy their cigarettes by the carton, and as far as holidays go they prefer both Mother's and Father's Day to either Christmas or Thanksgiving.

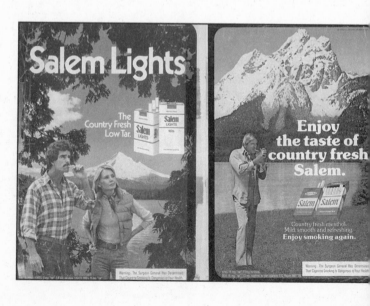

MALE NAMES
Stan, Dave, Brandon, Tyler, Nathan, Daniel

FEMALE NAMES
Chloe, Julia, Ashley, Lauren, Nicole

OCCUPATIONS
Health care specialist for Geico, *Reader's Digest* advertising sales rep, dental hygienist, mortuary driver, commercial real estate investor, rabbi

AGE RANGE
34–57

AWARDS AND PRIZES
Goldman Sachs foundation prize for excellence, the Google Da Vinci Code Quest finalist (one of ten thousand), third-place finish in fifth-grade spelling bee, MSNBC junior science achievement notice

RELIGION
Anglican, Lutheran, Reformed Presbyterian, Evangelical, Charismatic, Baptist, Methodist, Nazarene, Anabaptist, and Pentecostal

EDUCATION
College degrees in general with a smattering of postgraduate dabbling

SALARY RANGE
$110,000

LAST BOOK READ
Windows XP for Dummies (2nd ed.) by Andy Rathbone

A Ten-Day Smoking Program

How to Start Smoking Cigarettes

You've decided, even though the media, your friends, and your family are against it, to start smoking cigarettes. Is it possible, truly possible, to join the legions of happy cigarette smokers and stay there? Sure! If you carefully read over this program and do everything that is asked of you, you can be sure that within two to three weeks' time you will be a carefree smoker for good.

Learning how to smoke is hard work. Here's how the program will work for you. Finding trigger points that inspire you to smoke, such as which of your friends and family and what particular places and things trigger your urge, is what you'll initially look for. Then you will establish your habit and be on your way.

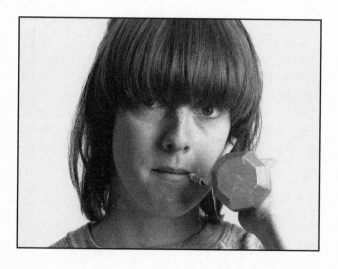

The program works as follows:

Days 1–4. These are the days of preparation. You'll begin by learning when you want to smoke cigarettes, and when you should be smoking. You'll ask yourself, Why haven't I been smoking? You'll start the rudimentary steps of developing a successful habit.

Days 5–8. The preparatory stage is over and the next four days are the establishing period. You will still refer to your reminder list and the 5 Ws (see below), but by day eight you will be on your own.

Days 9–10. Like a fledgling bird learning to fly, you will now be cast out into society with your cigarettes. Continually reinforcing your habit will be the focus. Pointers on maintenance after the ten days will be highlighted.

Days 1-2

Here's what you'll learn the first two days:

- You will test yourself to see what kind of smoker you would like to be.
- You will draw up a reminder list of reasons why you want to smoke.
- You will start a cigarette buying program for yourself.
- You will begin recording your cigarettes.

Reminder List

Draw up a list of reasons you want to smoke cigarettes (examples include: to look cool, to spend your idle time more wisely, to join your friends who are standing outside, etc.). Go from the ridiculous to the absurd to the practical. Write each reason on a separate sheet of paper. After you finish your task, number them in order of importance. This will be your reminder list. Carry it with you (it will fit nicely in your wallet or purse) and refer to it frequently.

Buying Program

Investigate the areas around your home and office for convenient places to buy cigarettes. Look at the values on the Internet. Find after-hours cigarette machines and supermarkets where you can conveniently make multicarton buys. Buy a few cartons of your favorite cigarettes and a few cartons of menthol, nonfilter, and varying filter. Leave these cartons around your home or private office in areas where you can see them easily. Buy a large supply of ashtrays, matches (wooden and book), and lighters. Keep them in your pockets and in the areas mentioned above. Remember, you want to be a smoker, so act like one.

Record Your Cigarettes

On a clipboard, which you will carry on your person during the first four days of this ten-day program, begin a daily tally sheet. Record each cigarette you smoke. Record the time, where you are, your activity, whom you are with, and finally your mood. The "Remarks" column could include such poignant observations as "great," "tasted good," "want another," and so on.

Smoking Triggers

Like any other habit, cigarette smoking has to be learned and practiced before it comes naturally. A good example of a habit would be saying grace before a meal. As a child, you were constantly reminded to do this by your parents, but soon the activity became so well established in the eating ritual that you did it naturally. It's the same with cigarettes, and the triggers move the habit along. Make a list of actions, activities, or situations where you think a cigarette will work and help. To help you, here are a few obvious and not so obvious smoking triggers.

- After a luscious meal with piping-hot coffee
- After a steamy sexual encounter

- Upon receiving yet another round of highballs in a smoky piano bar and going outside for a breath of fresh air
- Stepping off a packed elevator after an arduous day of work
- Being introduced at your first fraternity party to that "hottie" you have been dreaming about
- Waiting at the bus stop
- Coming out of a movie theater
- Right after the announcement has been made over the loudspeaker that your airplane will be delayed for three and a half hours

Shallow Breathing Exercise

When you become a habitual smoker you'll want to save your deep breaths for ushering the tobacco-enriched air into your lungs. Shallow breathing is good for between cigarettes. Once again, practice makes perfect.

Shallow breathing can be done anywhere, at any time, in the convenience of your home or office or amidst a crowd. It's easy, and here's how it's done:

1. Breathe only through your nose, not your mouth.
2. Bring the air only as far as your throat. Do not use your diaphragm.
3. Inhale quickly and exhale quickly.
4. You'll know you're doing it right if you can hear the air rushing in and out of your nose.

Days 3–4

Here's what you'll learn and do these next two days:

- The beginnings of your smoking pattern will be established.

🚬 You will begin substituting those time-wasting alternatives like gum chewing or crossword puzzles with cigarette smoking.

🚬 Analyze your tally sheets.

Smoking Patterns

Don't think that just because you have decided to become a cigarette smoker that it will come naturally and you'll just be a smoker. It will take planning, practice, and persistence. There are three ways of establishing your smoking pattern:

1. Begin eliminating silly alternatives in favor of smoking. Sports and physical activities should be avoided during this commencement period. If you enjoy crossword puzzles, skip them: They are a waste of time. Anything that indulges your hands, like crocheting or writing, is simply stealing precious smoking time.

2. If you don't have them you can't smoke them. Begin carrying several packs on your person with plenty of matches. Leave open packs around as reminders, offer cigarettes, and encourage those around you to smoke along with you.

3. To support your program, start going where good smokers can be found. Outside nightclubs, discos, and bars come to mind. Any designated smoking areas where the dedicated smokers are.

Time-Wasting Alternatives

Avoid the following activities and foods for the next few days, just to get your mind ready for the new cigarette smoking habit.

doodling
polishing your glasses
deep breathing (without a cigarette)

140

crossword puzzles
sports in general
jogging and running
drinking water
swimming, bathing, and showering
fresh fruits and vegetables
sugarless gum and carrot sticks
fruit juices and diet soda
calisthenics
hobby and church activities
brushing your teeth

Tally Sheets

At the end of your fourth day, take a good look at your tally sheets. Note the times you had a cigarette. Were there any periods when you went for over an hour without a cigarette? Why? When was your first? Your last? Could you make that extra effort to get up an hour earlier to fit in a few more in the morning? Will you stay up an hour or two later than usual to cap the evening off properly with a steady stream of cigarettes? Where did you smoke your cigarettes? Were you outside so much that your mind got distracted? Were you too busy with some other activity to smoke? Who were you with? Did you smoke mostly alone? If so, start smoking with other people more. Did your moods vary, did they travel the emotional rainbow using cigarettes as punctuation? Moods and reasons to the good smoker are irrelevant.

Continue showing your tally sheets to everyone as actual proof of your achievement.

"Look how many cigarettes I smoked today! I hope to top this number by five or ten tomorrow."

Days 5-6

Now that the preparatory stage is over, we are about to begin the establishment period. Things to remember from the first four days and to continue doing: shallow breathing between each cigarette, avoiding excessive exercise, buying your cigarettes in large quantities and often (single packs from various sources as well as multicarton buys), avoiding all hygienic habits. Discontinue your tally sheets as you enter this new period. Keep the sheets as a testament.

Here are the actions for today and tomorrow:

- Settle in with a favorite brand.
- Try doubling your consumption by having two at a time instead of only one.
- Step up your coffee and liquor intake.
- Begin establishing permanent friendships with fellow smokers.
- Smoke your cigarettes down as far as you can.
- Establish a separate bank account to support your cigarette habit.
- Notify all your close friends and relatives in writing that you are participating in a smoking program and that you hope soon to be a habitual smoker.

Days 7–8

These are the last two days of the establishing period and perhaps the hardest. The decision is now yours. The questions to ask yourself continuously are what we commonly refer to as the 5 Ws.

Whom do I smoke with?
What do I want to smoke cigarettes for?
When do I want to smoke cigarettes?
Where do I want to smoke cigarettes?
Why do I want to smoke cigarettes?

A good smoker can answer each of the 5 Ws honestly and at length. Ask yourself each of these questions as you light up each cigarette.

The action plan for days 7 and 8 is:

- ✌ Put the 5 Ws to work for you.
- ✌ Begin inhaling deeply and holding the smoke in your lungs as long as possible.
- ✌ Regardless of where you are, if you want a cigarette, light up and face the consequences later.
- ✌ Empty the ashtrays frequently.
- ✌ Buy yourself a several fancy lighters: one for the office, a butane coffee-table model for home, and a rainbow of BICs to carry on your person.
- ✌ Other smoking paraphernalia may heighten your pride as a smoker. Monogrammed cigarette cases, T-shirts of your favorite brand, or a scrapbook of advertisements of your favorite brand may subliminally work on your ego.

The establishing period is over. Now you have to do it on your own.

Days 9–10

Welcome aboard, smoker! You've made it to the elite club of cigarette smokers. It took willpower, persistence, and—you got it—guts. You've got a new habit and you should be proud of yourself. If you are half as determined as we think you are, the habit is going to become permanent. These last two days of the program will only help to reinforce the habit. Here's what we'll try to learn in the maintenance period:

- ✌ Idle hands are the devil's workshop.
- ✌ Be sure to have plenty of cigarettes on hand.

- Each morning, plan out your day with cigarettes.
- If you do exercise, reward yourself with cigarettes afterward.

Idle Hands

If you're having trouble convincing your hands to work with you in the program, then punish them by having a cigarette in your hand at all times. After a few days, your hands will miss the mere presence of a cigarette. Don't worry, hands have a way of learning on their own terms. Practice lighting matches in new ways. Play with your lighters, practice opening cartons and packages of cigarettes. Keep your ashtrays clean.

Cigarettes on Hand

Write to the manufacturers of your favorite brand and tell them about this program and yourself. You'll no doubt get a congratulatory reply with perhaps a carton of cigarettes as a token of gratitude. Stop into your local tobacconist and advise him to be well stocked. Keep cigarettes well in view. Open the packs. This heightens appetite and is easier for everyone in the long run.

Planning

Review your day each morning with coffee and cigarettes. Do you have enough cigarettes? Should you get

144

more? Whom will you see today? Are they smokers? If the answer is yes, bring extra cigarettes along. Do you foresee crises, long sitting periods, or will you be caught in a forbidden area for any length of time? Make a tip sheet and review your reminder list from day 1.

Exercise

Exercise can be slowly worked back into your life, but not too quickly. The key here is a reward system.

Watching exercise can be better for the cigarette smoker than actually participating. Watch a doubleheader on television at home with your cigarettes. You'll experience the competition and action and, guess what—you can smoke cigarettes at the same time.

Day 10 is the last day of the program, but you are not alone. You now have a new buddy. A buddy that will see you through thick and thin, a buddy that will get you through rough decisions as well as help you celebrate. Your new buddy will mark time for you, make your coffee taste better, help you talk on the telephone, win bowling and golf games for you, and heighten your enjoyment of television. Your new buddy will win you friends outside taverns and the office, burn up that excessive energy, and seemingly punctuate every task you set your mind to. Your new buddy, of course, is your cigarette.

The English speedboat racer Betty Carstairs arriving in New York aboard a luxury liner. She went on to Detroit to enter the speedboat races there. The reason the picture is included here is that it shows what complete confidence Ms. Carstairs has in herself and her cigarette. The total grip on her cigarette case, the nunlike collar, the starched handkerchief in the top pocket, and she was a speedboat racer!

Start feeling better about yourself now. Be determined that you want to be a smoker in the world and stick to your guns.

Good luck and congratulations!

"It's easy to quit smoking. I've done it hundreds of times."

—Mark Twain

Did You Know?

"I'm sure the tobacco companies loved *Basic Instinct.* One of them even launched a brand of 'Basic' cigarettes not long after the movie became a worldwide hit, perhaps inspired by my cigarette-friendly work. My movie made a lot of money; so did their new cigarette."

—Joe Eszterhas,
New York Times August 9, 2002

Smokingdate.com

It has gotten to this. An Internet dating service for cigarette smokers.

So obviously I found this site surfing around looking for what was going on in the world of cigarette smoking. It is a typical site, with questions about what you like to do in your free time (skydiving?) and the height of the person you would like to meet, and then there is the legitimate question that justifies the existence of the site: What is your preferred cigarette? So my question is, when all this personal information goes into their Wizard of Oz system, does it indeed take into account the type of cigarette you smoke? Does it evaluate the possibility of a Chesterfield smoker being compatible with a Salem smoker?

Okay, so I put in all the info and said to myself, why not see what it yields. I tried the chat room first and up came PREMIUM MEMBERS ONLY! Hmmm. Next was instant messaging, and again in big bold letters: PREMIUM MEMBERS ONLY! Who were the Premium Members? . . . *They must be people living in Virginia near the tobacco fields, heavy-duty smokers who rotate their brands and live in smoke zones, special suburban tracts that allow only smokers to live there and . . .*

Then I came out of my tobacco-driven dream state and realized that this, alas, was just another Web site and a way of capitalizing on the oldest (think Adam and Eve, a coed at the University of Nebraska searching the message board, Paris Hilton waiting for the phone to ring) and yet most modern of all of man's interests: relationships, the opposite sex, how to get a date—and it was using the cigarettes as the lure.

Television

The last cigarette TV commercial, featuring a suave madam and her Virginia Slims, ran on *The Tonight Show with Johnny Carson* on January 1, 1971, at exactly 11:59 p.m. Over, kaput, the end of an era. Television certainly had a good run with cigarettes, but before I get into a little cursory history of ads on TV, I want to raise two questions: whether Johnny Carson could smoke on the air after the last ad ran, sit there with his guests and work on his Winston, and second, did Ed McMahon smoke?

Cigarette companies were some of the first to advertise with aggressive panache on television. The big smoking guys had deep pockets and could afford to gamble on television, which in the 1940s and 1950s was still a doubtful medium in many people's minds and a new advertising playground. About everybody and their brother smoked then, so why not take a shot.

America's first regular television news program, *Camel News Caravan*, first aired in 1949 and was sponsored by Camel Cigarettes, and featured an ashtray on the desk in front of a little-seen newscaster, John Cameron Swayze, who was smoking Camels and had the Camel logo behind him.

But then the cigarette companies got a little more subtle, they product placed: the people on the shows or the programs smoked the cigarettes of the sponsors. For example, at the end of an episode of *I Love Lucy*, Desi asks for a cigarette and Lucy happily produces a pack of Philip Morris. She confides to the television audience, "You see how easy it is to keep a man happy?"

John Wayne pitched Camels on TV, "Mild and good tasting pack after pack. And I know, I've been smokin' 'em for twenty years"; and a host of people, including Robert Cummings and Garry Moore, pledged, "Winstons taste good like a cigarette should." There was a dancing Old Gold package, and people broke their Benson & Hedges because of their length.

> **"Smoking kills. If you're killed, you've lost a very important part of your life."**
> —Brooke Shields

The Flintstones, a cartoon show brought to us by Winston, featured smoking on the air. Fred and Wilma both smoked and even drank beer, and there wasn't a lot of complaining by the public about the fact that they smoked and carried on like everyone else in America at the time. Then in 1963 Pebbles was born, and the proud parents, Fred and Wilma, suddenly flushed the Winstons and Winston dropped the show. No way Winston was going to sponsor a prehistoric cartoon sitcom with a newly born baby.

In the late sixties, cigarette companies portrayed smokers as motivated, active, and loyal—an apple-pie-looking man or woman with a black eye would proclaim, "Us Tareyton smokers would rather fight than switch"; hairy-chested lumberjacks imparted, "Me and my Winstons, we got a real good thing"; station-wagon-driving Marlboro smokers urged "Come to where the flavor is"; while Camel smokers dressed in desert sands caravan khakis pledged, "I would walk a mile for a Camel."

The advertising ban in 1971 was expected to be devastating for the networks—but they have done all right since then in spite of immediately losing $220 million a year in revenues.

Cigarettes and the Armed Forces

Cigarettes have for the most part been a soldier's best friend for a long long time. French and English soldiers serving in eastern Europe during the Crimean War during the 1850s were introduced to cigarettes by the Spanish. The cigarettes they smoked were easy to carry, easy to light, and easy to smoke. After the war, the soldiers carted their new form of tobacco back to their native lands.

Cigarette smoking before the First World War was not popular and was infrequently seen. A few brands were marketed, but the majority of cigarettes smoked were of the roll-your-own variety. The ability to roll a cigarette, particularly with one hand, was considered not only an art but a skilled accomplishment.

Cigarettes were distributed free in the First World War. Major brands prepared for war and sought out and established a market because of the war. In 1918, the U. S. government requisitioned the manufacture of Bull Durham tobacco for the war effort. Sending cigarettes to the boys on the front was considered one of the highest priorities of the war effort.

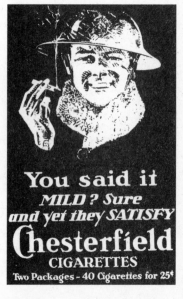

With the First World War in full swing, Chesterfield took advantage of it by featuring doughboys in their advertisements.

The thinking perhaps was that the cigarettes would inspire the soldiers as they sat there trying to manipulate the complex rifles and cannons they had been issued—inspire them in the sense that America was behind them and now they were men! But cigarettes didn't come without dangers. Any light coming from or seen in the trenches spelled death. Lighting a cigarette became an art, and the soft glow of a cigarette needed to be carefully guarded. Cigarettes nevertheless became many a soldier's best friend as they sat out the grueling hours of loneliness in the rain-soaked foxholes and dugouts.

Can you hitchhike across the country using nothing but cigarettes for money? Sponsors of a popular television show in the 1950s staked discharged serviceman Hiram Sizemore of Manchester, Kentucky, with thirty cartons of cigarettes in Hollywood and sent him on his way in his civies to see if he could make it back to his ol' Kentucky home with a banjo on his knee—no, wait, wrong song. Nevertheless, ol' Hiram indeed got back home.

One popular slogan for Chesterfield cigarettes was "They do satisfy." Cigarette companies began using pictures of soldiers smoking cigarettes in their advertising, and lots of people regarded soldiers as heroes. So, when they saw the soldiers smoking, they started smoking too.

Cigarette companies realized that women were not smoking as much as men, so since the ad campaigns with soldiers smoking worked, they started featuring women in ads. One famous ad for Lucky Strike cigarettes read, "I light a Lucky and go light on the sweets." Cigarette companies sold women on the fact that if they smoked cigarettes, they would not gain weight. "That's how I keep in shape and always look peppy."

During the Second World War, three main things went together: pin-ups, cigarettes, and soldiers. Drawings and photographs of appealing women, like Raleigh's "The Pride of the Regiment," were seen in the wall lockers of most stateside World War II servicemen. It seemed the entire armed forces smoked. Used coffee cans painted and labeled "Butts" were placed around barracks. On the parade ground cigarette butts had to be fieldstripped. A messy or wasteful soldier was frowned upon, and punishment for simply tossing cigarettes would include things like having to police an entire area (usually around the entire barracks area or the marching fields), picking up every piece of scrap around. A cigarette is fieldstripped when the smoker splits what is left of the cigarette paper lengthwise, shakes the tobacco free, then wads the paper up into a tiny ball (see page 67). Fieldstripped cigarettes are not noticeable.

There were few pleasures for the foot soldier in combat, but one of them was smoking cigarettes. Field rations consisted of canned meats, a can of fruit, vitamin-fortified biscuits, plus a small accessory packet containing chewing gum, coffee, sugar, toilet paper, a book of matches, and of course cigarettes. There were several versions or revisions of C rations issued during the Second World War. Toward the end, a soldier's daily rations included a cigarette pack with nine cigarettes in it, or three smaller packs of three cigarettes each. Chesterfield, Lucky Strike, and Old Gold were three World War II C-ration cigarette brands that had very plain packets devoid of graphics.

Once again the ad boys run in and capitalize on the war.

Prior to being sent overseas, World War II soldiers and sailors were stationed at U.S. bases outside the continental borders, where they received advanced training. Tax-exempt cigarettes were sold to these servicemen at their Post or Base Exchanges. Camels, Luckies, and Chesterfields cost five cents a pack or fifty cents a carton, but there could be a string attached. In order to buy one carton of their preferred brand at the Puunene Naval Air Station Exchange on the Hawaiian island of Maui, smokers also had to buy two cartons of an off-brand cigarette. When it was time for a serviceman to ship out, oftentimes these cartons of unwanted cigarettes were left in wall or foot lockers for the less discriminating.

The C-ration cigarettes that were issued during the Vietnam War were almost identical to the sample packs of four that tobacco sales reps handed out to the public. The only difference was the U.S. tax-exempt notice printed on the side of the box. Pall Mall, Winston, and Benson & Hedges Menthol were three of the brands smoked by military personnel sent to fight in Southeast Asia. Soldiers, sailors, and marines who were nonsmokers traded their cigarettes for either the can of peaches or the packet to make hot cocoa. C-ration cigarettes were discontinued in 1972.

What war is this? The snapshot was probably taken in Florida.

During the lingering Iraqi war, the Department of Defense no longer provides tobacco to the men and women they send to fight the enemies of the United States. One particular photograph that grabbed the nation's attention showed a serviceman with a cigarette between his lips. The hundreds of newspapers across the country that ran a copy of the picture received an enormous amount of flack from the general public. The anti-tobacco people felt the picture of the young soldier sent out the wrong message, and thus the modern smoking soldier was a poor role model for anyone who was supportive of the war. A reader of the *New York Post* suggested: "Maybe showing a marine in a tank, helping another GI or drinking water would have a more positive impact on your readers."

Did You Know?

A 1968 poll taken among smokers revealed (in order of the number of times mentioned) why people smoked cigarettes: sociability, fragrance, relaxation, stimulation, steady nerves, smoothness, quiet hunger, sight of the smoke, feel of the lips, feel of the hands, and finally . . . taste.

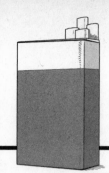

Winston Profile

Winston smokers are ubiquitous. They can be found hanging around country-club swimming pool snack bars as well as guiding eighteen-wheelers over the Donner Pass in blizzards. Winstons are purely American. Norman Rockwell and Babe Ruth would have smoked Winstons while they drank Cokes at the Fourth of July parade. Winston smokers are generous and gregarious; they are always willing to give someone a cigarette as well as bum one. They are in general a satisfied lot in that their brand is available everywhere. They are known to experiment with new foods, don't worry about skipping breakfast, and prefer to drive SUVs with imitation wood on the side if it is available. In the fall they watch the World Series together in crewneck sweaters, use an occasional swear word (mostly with disobedient pets), and they watch *Animal House* over and over because they could swear they were there.

MALE NAMES
Greg, Charley, Evan, Kenneth, Lloyd, Patrick, David, Stephen

FEMALE NAMES
Alice, Catherine, Eden, Holly, Jessica, Melissa, Stephanie, Wendy

OCCUPATIONS
Priest, politician (state and local levels), suburban housewife, college student with an eye on low fat cafeteria selections, art dealer, librarian, real estate dabbler, Estee Lauder salesperson (part-time, no weekends), rare furniture restorer

AGE RANGE
30–55

AWARDS AND PRIZES
Door prize at St. Mary's Thanksgiving turkey shoot, attending a NASA space shuttle takeoff after a spirited visit to Disney World, limbo finalist at Club Med in Aruba, coordinating chairman of the Jewel Ball in Kansas City, BMOC nominee at Michigan State

RELIGION
Catholic, Christian (no Bible thumpers, though), a sprinkling of atheists

EDUCATION
A college degree achieved in four years

SALARY RANGE
$70,000–$175,000

LAST BOOK READ
It's Not About the Bike by Lance Armstrong

Little Lady Lighting Her Eve

Learning to light and smoke an Eve cigarette requires not only poise but grace, that certain little woman's touch. After all, you're about to enter that special garden of flavor created just for you. Pretty package, individually designed floral filter, and the delicious taste of specially blended tobaccos all add up to one thing: Eve cigarettes. Now here is the method:

Begin the process by grasping your lighter in your right hand and a fresh package of Eves in your left.

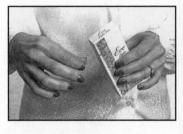

Set your lighter down and remove the cellophane strip from the gaily adorned package.

Gently open the lid on your handy "box" of Eve Lights 120's.

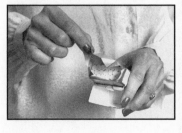

Remove the protective aluminum foil sealer and place it in the proper trash receptacle.

With your left hand grasping the base of the box, remove a single cigarette with your right hand.

Place the cigarette box on a table with your left hand. With your now free left hand, grab your lighter. Your right hand should be bringing your unlit cigarette toward your mouth. Insert the cigarette between your lips.

Flick your lighter to ignite the cigarette, inhale, and you have begun your journey to pleasure.

" Remember, if you smoke after sex you're doing it too fast. "
—WOODY ALLEN

Those Darn Candy Cigarettes

For some reason, more than a hundred years ago some capitalizing confectioners (they being candy makers), began creating a host of chocolate, candy, and bubble gum items that resembled cigarettes. Their target market was children no doubt. The major cigarette manufacturers paid them little or no mind; they were swimming in money from all the cigarettes they sold to adults. They did take a little note in insuring that the reproductions were "good" reproductions.

The American public believes or wants to believe that these candy cigarettes have been outlawed. They have not been. The creators of these little delights have just stayed one step ahead of the government's long arm of justice and started producing them off shore (just like everything else in America), to avoid hassles, and to keep them hidden from the public eye.

What is funny, ironic, however you want to put it, is that the companies who make and market candy cigarettes will slightly alter the names of their products but still retain the graphic styles of specific cigarette packages. Or they will completely leave the tobacco launch pad and create something anew; thus, names like "Little Bob Dog" or "Castle" or "Palm." The list below consists of some of the thousands of types of candy cigarettes. They are not available everywhere, only in select shopping arenas, and of course online: ENTER: 3 Cartons of Popeye Candy Sticks. SEND and REMIT.

A few candy cigarette names:

Acmel

Winstun

Sombrero

Future10

Viseroy

Salam

Popeye Tasty Candy
    Sticks*

Kemt

Old Toad

Target

Raleyg

Princess

Stallion

---

*A result of the fear that cigarettes may be smoked by children; thus, not Popeye Cigarettes but Popeye Candy Sticks. The product itself is the same size as a cigarette, white with simulated filters. In case you ever did light one, they burned kind of like marshmallows and the fumes tasted like an Almond Joy.

One-Hand Johnny

An old favorite among young soldiers, college students, and busy guys working the pits at NASCAR races is lighting a match from a matchbook with only one hand. Looks easy, but it requires a lot of practice. An expert can do it anywhere, anytime. The extreme example is the yellow-coated Marlboro cowboy whose one hand is expertly guiding a husky Appaloosa through Montana snow drifts in a forty-five-mile-an-hour gale, while the other hand is busy lighting one of the dozens of cigarettes he will have before he makes it home to his Circle K ranch.

Here are the six basic steps:

1. With your right hand, grasp the book of matches with your thumb placed firmly on the matchbook lid.

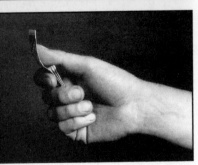

2. Slip the matchbook lid open with your thumb. Grasp the base of the book with your index and second fingers.

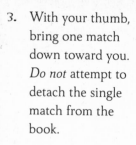

3. With your thumb, bring one match down toward you. *Do not* attempt to detach the single match from the book.

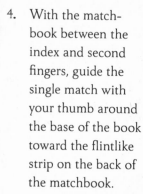

4. With the matchbook between the index and second fingers, guide the single match with your thumb around the base of the book toward the flintlike strip on the back of the matchbook.

5. Flick the match head upward with your thumb. Your pad will naturally form a cap. The ignited match, because of the tensile strength of the material, with flip free and be ignited.

> "But he can't be a man because he doesn't smoke the same cigarettes as me."

—FROM "(I CAN'T GET NO) SATISFACTION"
BY MICK JAGGER AND KEITH RICHARDS

An Old Indian Tradition

An old Indian tradition has it that a Swedish minister once took it upon himself to inform the chiefs of the Susquehanna Indians, in a kind of sermon, of the principal historical facts on which the Christian religion is founded, and particularly the fall of Adam and Eve.

When he had finished, he was addressed by an old Indian orator, thusly: "What you have told us is very good; we thank you for coming so far to tell us those stories you have heard from your mothers. In return we will tell you what we have heard from ours.

"In the beginning we had only the flesh of animals to eat. If the hunters failed, we starved. Two of our hunters, having killed a deer and broiled a part of it, saw a young woman descend from the clouds, and seat herself on a hill hard by. Said one to the other: 'It is a spirit, perhaps, that has smelt our venison; let us offer some of it to her.'

"They accordingly went about slicing the deer and gave her the tongue. She was pleased with its flavor and said: 'Your kindness shall be rewarded. Come here thirteen moons hence, and you shall find your rewards.'

"They did so and found maize and kidney beans growing where the young woman's left hand had been, and where she had sat they found *tobacco.*"

"Do you mind if I don't smoke?"
—GROUCHO MARX

Waiflike model Kate Moss holding a lit cigarette and situated squarely in a permanent state of ennui. (Rose Hartman/Time Life Pictures/Getty Images)

Weight Loss

A handy way of losing weight would be to start smoking cigarettes. It's no secret that those extra pounds sneak up on you when you haven't maintained a daily smoking habit.

One of the first physical phenomena you will notice when you start smoking heavily is a loss of smell and taste. Good. Those two senses make you want to eat. With the insertion of nicotine into the body, and the toxic effects thereof, the gastrointestinal tract's yearning is satisfied without having to stuff it with saltine crackers, diet root beer, and sardines. You will feel worse but you *will* lose weight. Instead of nibbling away on Planters mixed nuts like a field mouse or darting back and forth from the refrigerator for Häagen-Dazs toffee yogurt or chicken enchilada dip, grab a cigarette, light up, and enjoy full pleasure without gaining weight.

A few things to keep in mind during those first few weeks when you have just started your weight-loss smoking program:

1. Carry lots of matches and cigarettes (loose or in the pack) in all your pockets.
2. When you feel good, you are gaining weight, so light up and stop the process.
3. Remember that craving a cigarette is something that is developed. Remind yourself to smoke. Put Post-its up around the house and in your car with the word "Smoke" on them.
4. Hang around with heavy smokers.
5. Don't eat, smoke.

Good luck! And remember, if you feel good, you're gaining weight.

Blowing Smoke

One cold and windy night in West Hollywood, three guys are arrested in an adult bookstore. They are brought down to the police station, booked, and then released on their own recognizance with the proviso being that all three of them are to report to court three days later. Three days later they all show up at the appointed courtroom and appear before the judge. He asks the first guy to stand.

"What is your name?" he asks.

"John," the guy answers.

"Why were you arrested?" the judge asks.

"Well, I was by the magazine rack smoking a cigarette and blowing smoke," he answers.

The judge doesn't see any infraction of the law, so he dismisses the guy. He then calls up the next one.

"What's your name?" he asks.

"John," the guy replies.

"And why were you arrested?" the judge asks.

"I was by the magazine rack holding a cigarette and blowing smoke," he answers.

Again, the judge sees nothing offensive. *This so-called adult store is beginning to sound more like a smoking club!* he thinks. So he dismisses the charges against the second guy and calls up the third guy.

"What's your name? No, wait, let me guess: John," the judge says.

"No," says the guy, "my name is Smoke."

Tobacco as a Crop

Tobacco as a crop rapidly exhausts the soil in which it is grown. An American early tobacco planter was required to either refertilize his soil and let it lay fallow for a season as the nutrients sank in or to clear new land for planting. The latter proved to be cheaper and easier. This practice led to the formation of very large estate/plantations and required, as is obvious perhaps, a large supply of cheap labor to maintain the land. In the beginning, indentured servants from England had been the main source of this cheap labor, but by the 1660s, not only had the servant population declined, but the prisoner population in England had been depleted as well. The demand for cheap labor had simply outgrown the supply.

In 1672, the Royal African Company of London was granted a monopoly in the slave trade. Between 1680 and 1686, the company transported an average of five thousand slaves a year. Between 1680 and 1688, it sponsored 249 voyages to Africa.

Rival English merchants were not amused with this monopoly. In 1698, Parliament yielded to their demands and opened the slave trade to all. With the end of the monopoly, the number of slaves transported on English ships would increase dramatically—to an average of over twenty thousand a year.

These black slaves that who were brought to America were primarily used in the tobacco trade. They worked the land and became commonly known as "field hands."

Did You Know?

Cigarettes are the most heavily advertised product in the United States. The tobacco companies spend $4 billion a year, or $11 million a day, to try to get people to buy cigarettes.

People Who Never Smoked Cigarettes

Jesus
Dakota Fanning
Michael Bloomberg
Kanye West
Mohandas Karamchand Gandhi
Roy Rogers
Annette Bening
Lou Gehrig
Jimmy Carter
Beck
Oprah Winfrey
Adolf Hitler*

All of these people have always been perceived as being so *nice* and so unencumbered that it is impossible to think they ever partook or will partake in the future of the joys of tobacco.

---

*Adolf Hitler was a smoker from 1897–1924. However, he is included on this list because a recently invented myth is circulating by tobacco apologists that he was a nonsmoker! More than half a century after his death, this myth has been invented by people, all of whom I'm sure have a mighty sharp ax to grind. I would imagine they truly believe that the real truth has been forgotten and hope that people will buy into the new fact they have created: Hitler was an avid nonsmoker and never thought his blemish-free Arian race would step so low as to smoke cigarettes.

Epilogue

Secondary Smoke

In 1983, I wrote and published a book called *The Joys of Smoking Cigarettes*. The editor who signed the book up was a smoker, the head of the sales department at the publisher smoked, I had a girlfriend who smoked, and they sold cigarettes for under five dollars a pack at my local pub. Everything seemed rosy and smokey. Then my editor decided to leave the publishing business before the book was completed and I was assigned a new editor, a nonsmoker. My smoking girlfriend left, and my new assistant at work turned out to be a nonsmoker who frowned on the practice. My task with my new editor became like trying to explain an iPod to Edgar Allan Poe. "Why exactly are you writing this book?" he once asked me. "For the pure joy," I replied, "for the pure joy."

Now, nearly thirty years later, the joys are still the same, but the cigarette smoking world has changed, just a tad. In 1983, for example, I could light up in my office or smoke on the long-distance trains or in restaurants and bars—today I am, along with the other cigarette smokers of the world, forced to put on my jacket, pick up my keys and wallet, and ride the elevator down to the lobby if I am in a high-rise or walk out the door if not, to smoke on the sidewalk in front of the building, all because someone came up with the notion that secondary smoke would be bad for their health or that it was an invasion of their privacy. And I might add that today I also pay about four times the previous amount for that pleasure. The spaces in which smoking is permitted have shrunk and smokers have been relegated to the sidewalk outside, public parks, always outside, and as a result, a close-knit club of smokers has arisen. Like biblical outcasts or lepers waiting at the village gates, we huddle together and smoke and complain and light each other's ciggies, compare brands, tell smoking stories; we're brothers and sisters, juvenile delinquents in black motorcycle jackets, children of the libertines, do-it-yourselfers with a happy dependency on a nasty habit. I've grown tighter and more loyal to the whole fraternity of it all, but it is, when I stop to think about it, a bit ridiculous.

Cover design, by Joy Taylor, for the first incarnation of *The Joys of Smoking Cigarettes*, published by Henry Holt in 1983. Yes, copies are available on eBay and can be seen at street fairs, country fairs, flea markets. Seems it was published back in the Punic War–era now, back when we could smoke at our leisure, listen to Ronald Reagan speeches, and not worry about our e-mail spam, our ATM passwords, and whether or not Lindsay Lohan will indeed get married before she is thirty.

We cigarette smokers are the victims of advertising—not now, obviously, because there is none. But someone way back in our lives smoked, an uncle, a parent, a rock star, and they were the victims and we just picked up the habit and nuance from them. When modern cigarettes first started being mass distributed around 1915, advertisers were the first to start pushing them with extensive billboard and magazine campaigns. Everywhere you turned then, you saw cigarette ads promising smokers that if they smoked a

Print ad for the "zesty" Misty cigarettes. See how the model's teeth, nails, the whites of her eyes, and the cigarette are all the same tone of white. So clean, so American. And the cigarettes themselves are slims (you won't gain wait if you smoke sixty or seventy of these a day, baby), they are menthol (the hint of coolness gives a girl that confidence she needs), and rounding out the adjective trifecta, they are lights (so health conscious and smart). No wonder they banned cigarettes in bars, with everyone sitting around smoking Mistys . . . "Hey, can I have one of your . . . Mistys?" "You know . . . these Mistys sure live up to their reputation, don't they, Albert?"

particular brand they could become rich, famous, liked, whatever. Then the campaigns spread to radio and then to television and then back to magazines. Movie stars, soldiers, housewives, doctors, whatever it took for the advertising industry to convince the gullible public that if you smoked, you were special. But now that is all over. The big tobacco companies have diversified and are selling everything from baby food to Depends and take little or no responsibility for the smoking habit. "We only make them, we don't smoke them."

This leaves us, the last of the breed, the smokers, lonesome as buffalo on the great prairies, the fifteenth-century dwarves forced to live in caves in the mountains, society's pariahs, to unite and be one. This new edition of the book is not for *them*, it is for *us*. It is for the hordes that flocked to movie theaters to see John

The new world of smoking. Does the staring woman even know he is smoking? Will she abandon him when she does find out? Does she smoke? Is that all she wants out of this a cigarette, or does she have more in mind? And where are they, in some foreign country? You can't smoke in bars here in the land of the free.

Turturro's *Romance and Cigarettes* and Jim Jarmusch's *Coffee and Cigarettes*, or the readers of Richard Klein's *Cigarettes are Sublime*, or the hilarious *Easy Way to Start Smoking* by George Cockerill and David Owen.

The numbers of smokers may be declining, but those of us who still do indulge are just getting better.

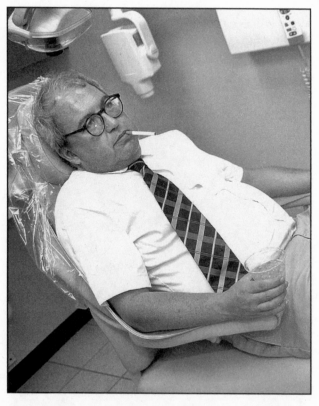

Around holiday time or other gala family occasions, journalist Scott Fitzgerald usually gets a full assortment of cigarettes a few days ahead for all guests involved. He gets a variety of Camels, filters in the box, Wides, and straights, along with some Salems or Kools. At the grocery store nearby where he lives, he has to request a store clerk to get his cigarettes. They are locked up because of the new laws to keep cigarettes away from minors. Recently, when he gave the store clerk his request, the suspicious clerk raised his eyebrow and asked, "Camel regulars. You mean the short ones?"

An Abbreviated Smoking and Cigarette Glossary

ashtray A receptacle used by smokers to deposit the ash and butts of cigarettes and cigars. **Ashtrays** are typically manufactured from glass, stoneware, porcelain, or metals, such as silver or aluminum; however, some are made of wood, marble, or clay. As part of a table setting during the 1950s and 1960s, small personal **ashtrays** were commonly placed on the top right-hand side, behind the wine and water glasses. Today they are considered antiques and sell on eBay.

bum Figuratively, a term meaning to borrow a cigarette; literally, though, "Can I have a cigarette?" A code among serious cigarette smokers, one **bums** and one gives and at the end of the day it probably works out to be about equal. Usage: "Hey, dude, can I **bum** a smoke?"

bust-down The act of giving one-half of a cigarette to someone after you have smoked the first half. This is also called **cutting**. It can also be used to describe the process of breaking an extremely long cigarette, like a Pall Mall or Chesterfield King, in half and in effect creating two cigarettes.

car cigarette lighter A device containing a thin coil of nichrome wire, through which very high current (15–20 amps) passes when the device is activated, usually by pushing its handle in. The heating element becomes glowing orange hot in seconds, and the handle pops out. Due to the decreasing popularity of smoking and the popularity of in-car electronics, the cigarette lighter has been replaced by a 12-volt power outlet that does not actually function to light cigarettes. Some minivans come with several lighter sockets, allowing various devices to be used at different seats.

cigarette holder A slender tube in which a single cigarette is held for smoking, as opposed to the cigarette case, which holds many cigarettes for the purpose of carrying them. Most frequently made of silver, jade, or Bakelite (popular in the past but now wholly replaced by modern plastics), cigarette holders were considered an essential part of ladies' fashion from the 1900s through the mid-1960s, and are still widely popular accessories in many aspects of Japanese fashion.

Cigarette Smoking Man (abbreviated to CSM) A fictional character played by William B. Davis on the 1993–2002 television series *The X-Files*.

Coffee and Cigarettes A 2003 independent film directed by Jim Jarmusch. The film consists of eleven short stories that share coffee and cigarettes as a common thread.

djarum A brand of clove cigarettes.

dick A name or term used when asking for the last drags of someone else's cigarette. Usage: "Can I smoke your dick?"

dings What "hip" teenagers in Canada call cigarettes.

Bob Dylan American singer-songwriter who attributed his voice change on his album *Nashville Skyline* to his quitting smoking, though this is disputed. He is seen reading a paper in the 1967 documentary *Don't Look Back*, where he quotes the journalist as saying he "smokes eighty a day."

Eve Cigarettes Cigarettes manufactured in the United States and Germany by the Liggett Group, the smallest of the major U.S. tobacco companies. They were introduced in 1971 as competition for rival Philip Morris's **Virginia Slims**, a cigarette targeted at the growing ladies' market. **Virginia Slims** were aimed at women who identified themselves as liberated, independent, and modern; **Eves** were aimed at women content to be feminine.

fag A British colloquialism for cigarette. Usage: "Could I bum a fag off you, mate?"

hot box A slang term used to describe when a smoker inhales rapidly, causing the cherry (burned end) to become unusually large.

Jewport A derogatory slang term for Newport cigarettes, indicating of course that those of the Hebrew persuasion prefer the robust taste of Newports.

Noblesse (Hebrew: מלבוג) An Israeli cigarette brand produced by Dubek, Israel's oldest cigarette manufacturer. The brand, launched in 1952 in a distinct green, 80mm, "softpack," which has never been dramatically changed, is the oldest in Dubek's product line. The cigarette also has the highest tar (19mg) and nicotine (1.3mg) amounts available on the Israeli massmarket.

"No Smoking" A cartoon made by the Walt Disney Company in 1951, featuring the ever-loving Goofy, who is in constant search throughout the film for a "smoke." A random search found no other meanings for this term.

Port A loose or one Newport cigarette. Usage: "Gimme one of dem phat Ports 'fore I talk to that hottie wit da body."

Premier A smokeless cigarette released in the United States in 1988 by the R. J. Reynolds Tobacco Company. It worked by heating and aerosolizing tobacco flavor and was intended to reduce or eliminate the unhealthy side effects associated with smoking, both to the smoker and to the people around the smoker. The cigarette took several years to develop at a cost of more than $1 billion. **Premier** was the subject of a subplot in the movie *Barbarians at the Gate* starring James Garner. It was withdrawn from the market in 1989, less than a year after its debut.

refries Partially smoked cigarettes that have been extinguished but can be relit and smoked again. Also called "butts."

rolling papers Small sheets, rolls, or leaves of paper that are sold for rolling one's own cigarettes either by hand or with a rolling machine. When rolling a cigarette, one fills the rolling paper with tobacco, shag, marijuana, or other herbs.

second-hand smoking Also known as involuntary smoking, passive smoking, or Environmental Tobacco Smoke, this happens when the smoke from one person's burning tobacco product (or the smoker's exhalation) is inhaled by others. Passive smoking is one of the key issues leading to smoking bans in workplaces, restaurants, and public places.

sissy sticks A commonly used term for cigarettes that nonsmokers use. Usage: "Hey, Margaret, put that sissy stick out and let's make a cake."

Slash A very hard-rocking lead guitarist, Slash plays right from his inner soul at times. His former bandmates of Guns N' Roses thought he might have been from outer space. Under his ubiquitous stove-pipe top hat, a forest of curly black hair, the heavily tinted sunglasses, and the ever-present burning cigarette suspended from his pursed lips, there is supposedly a very shy, handsome caring guy.

smoking caps Caps worn while smoking to stop the hair from smelling of smoke. They are similar to smoking jackets, though their use, even in Victorian times, was not necessarily as widespread.

smoking lamp A naval term designating that smoking is permitted. The smoking lamp is out or lit in specified spaces or throughout the ship; the term usually comes in the form of an announcement specifying where smoking is permitted or prohibited during certain hours or operations.

"The Smoking Peanut" A *SpongeBob SquarePants* episode from season two.

smurt The various remains of discarded cigarette butts that are gathered and rolled into a new cigarette.

spliff Originally, a Jamaican term for a large cone-shaped smoking device carved of wood and packed full of cannabis (possibly mixed with tobacco leaf [fronta] or pieces, as per one's taste). Eventually rolling papers replaced the solid cone. Bob Marley was a big spliff man.

suicide drag The very last possible drag before the cigarette burns down to the filter. The term came about because the smoker has an equal chance of ending up with a drag of tobacco smoke or inhaling the foul-tasting smoke from the burning filter.

tailors A term short for "tailor made," denoting that a cigarette was made by machine and not hand-rolled. It is a term used only in Australia and New Zealand.

tobacco smoking Often referred to as just "smoking." It is the act of burning the dried or cured leaves of the tobacco plant and inhaling the smoke for pleasure or ritualistic purposes, or more commonly out of habit and to satisfy addiction. The practice was common among the Plains Indians, and was later introduced to the rest of the world by sailors following European exploration of the Americas.

Frank Zappa American composer and musician who was renowned for his cigarette and coffee preferences, although he abstained from all other drugs. Zappa was quoted as saying that tobacco was his favorite "food." Cigarettes are referenced in the titles of two of his instrumentals, "It Must Be a Camel" and "Twenty Small Cigars," and mentions of smoking can also be found throughout his lyrics.

Acknowledgments

Writing thank-yous and acknowledging people for a book entitled *The Joys of Smoking Cigarettes* is a bit like handing a three-year-old a razor blade. Everything about this tome is taboo and seemingly bad for you. Smoking cigarettes is an expensive habit; it cuts life back; it alienates people; it is simply not allowed in so many places now; it's old-fashion noir coughy-coughy and so twentieth century; it smells; and it destroys curtains, couches, relationships, and the insides of cars. The list could go on exploring every alley of body, mind, and spirit, but the simple fact is a lot of people still do smoke cigarettes, and it is them that I am thanking and acknowledging as the boat pulls to shore. Thanks for not throwing the football into the crowd and quitting, for not sitting in the den falling asleep with the newspaper on your lap as family gathers in the doorway whispering "Doesn't he look good and healthy now that he quit smoking?"

On the practical side, thanks to Casey Kait, my original HarperCollins editor, to Will Hinton for guiding this book down the editorial/production line, and to my agent, Anne Reid Garrett, whose inspiration was that this project would close the door on my cigarette days and that I would lay tobacco down.

And thanks for everyone who had the stamina and a good sturdy pair of Tony Lamas to step up to the cash register in the bookstore with a copy or two of the book, or click "Put in Cart" on their computer, and make their statement to the world: I smoke cigarettes.

About the Author

JAMES FITZGERALD is the author of six books, including the *New York Times* bestseller *The First Family Paper Doll Cut-Out Book* (Dell, 1981). He has been a literary agent since 2000. Prior to being an agent he was an editor at Doubleday and St. Martin's Press.